WILD FLOWERS OF THE YORKSHIRE DALES

by

Sylvia M. Arnold

With photographs by

John M. Arnold

HUTTON PRESS

1988

Published by the Hutton Press Ltd.
130 Canada Drive, Cherry Burton, Beverley
East Yorkshire HU17 7SB

Printed and Bound by

Clifford Ward & Co. (Bridlington) Ltd.
55 West Street, Bridlington, East Yorkshire
YO15 3DZ

ISBN 0 907033 65 2

ACKNOWLEDGEMENTS

I am indebted to members of my wild flower classes in Hull from 1976 to 1986, and to those who came on our numerous, botanical field-trips to the Dales.

I would also like to thank my daughters and husband for their help in the preparation of the manuscript.

Sylvia Arnold
April 1988

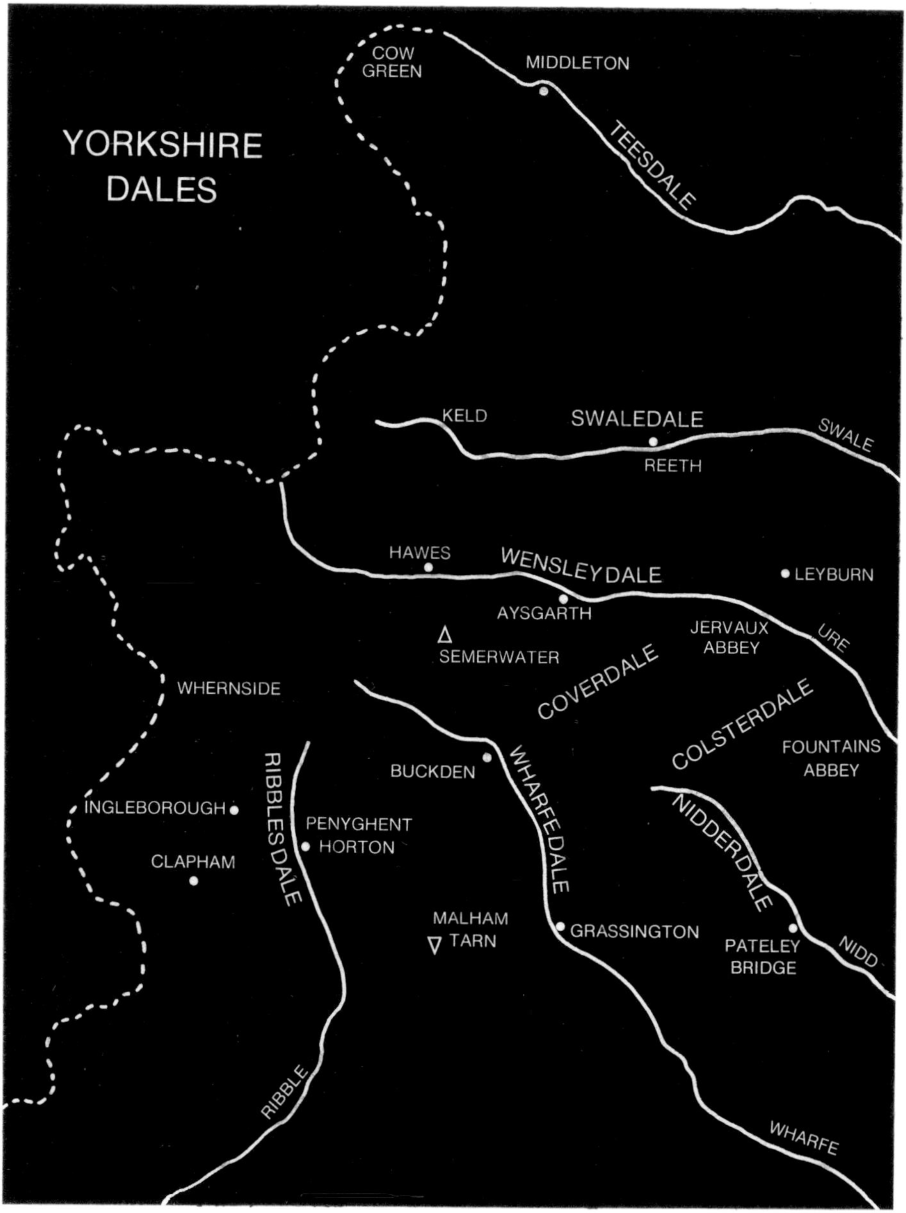

YORKSHIRE DALES
COW GREEN
MIDDLETON
TEESDALE
KELD
SWALEDALE
SWALE
REETH
HAWES
WENSLEYDALE
LEYBURN
AYSGARTH
JERVAUX ABBEY
URE
SEMERWATER
COVERDALE
WHERNSIDE
COLSTERDALE
FOUNTAINS ABBEY
BUCKDEN
WHARFEDALE
RIBBLESDALE
NIDDERDALE
INGLEBOROUGH
PENYGHENT
HORTON
CLAPHAM
MALHAM TARN
GRASSINGTON
PATELEY BRIDGE
NIDD
RIBBLE
WHARFE

LIST OF CONTENTS

Front cover: Globe-Flowers (Trollius europaeus)

INTRODUCTION

The Yorkshire Dales is limestone country, an upland area of high windswept fells and deep shaded valleys carrying streams and rivers that rush east to the lowlands and their ultimate destination — the North Sea. For the naturalist the Dales offer a dazzling kaleidoscope of wild flowers set against a backcloth of hillside and valley, mountain summit and riverside meadow. This is beautiful scenery where white rocks are set into emerald hillsides and crystal waters drop from sunlit dales into deep forbidding caverns. The countryside is infinitely varied, both in physical features, climatic extremes and the flora that roots in this soil and flowers under the welcoming sky. We have toiled up the slopes of Ingleborough in a shimmering July heat wave, and listened to tinkling ice fragments lapping the shores of Cow Green Reservoir, watched holiday-makers enjoying a calm Semerwater and gasped at the foaming spray of High Force in spate. The Dales offer the contrast between the busy streets of Hawes and the lonely crags above Littondale, between multitudes and solitude. The flowers of the Dales are equally diverse.

After the ice melted at the end of the last great ice-age some 10,000 years ago, the flowers of the countryside gradually returned to the north from the snow-free areas of the south of England and the Continent. The bed of the channel was dry at this time and remained a bridge for migrating animals and plants. With the melting of the great glaciers and snow fields, sea levels across the world rose and 7,000 years ago the channel was flooded, returning this country to its island status. By this time the deciduous forests had returned to the north of England. These trees shaded out the tiny alpine plants which had recolonised the landscape in the wake of the ice. Only where trees could not grow well did these tiny beautiful herbs persist. Many areas in the Dales offered a rocky refuge for this late glacial flora during the period of maximum forest development. These habitats remained in full sunshine and tiny alpines have flourished here for 9,000 years. Malham Cove (plate x) may be the most spectacular cliff on the Great Scar Limestone but every hillside has some rocky precipice where the blanket of trees was broken and sunshine streamed down to the ground. It is not surprising that the Dales are dotted with botanical rarities. The location of many are closely guarded secrets whispered among the ranks of natural history societies.

The purpose of this book is to encourage the holiday-maker to notice and value the unique wild flowers of the area, and suggest to the naturalist and rambler those areas that offer the most interesting wild habitats. My purpose is not to disclose the secret sites for rare flowers — the enthusiast will find these for himself. The range of rarities spans almost the whole vista of British habitat types from the white woodland bells of the Angular Soloman's Seal *(Polygonatum odorata)* to the saprophytic Coral Root Orchid *(Corallorhiza trifida)* on a quarry floor, or the Alpine Bartsia *(Bartsia alpina)* of calcareous wetland to the famed Lady's Slipper Orchid *(Cypripedium calceolaria)* on calcareous scree. These and other rarities were part of the late glacial flora, this and their need for good illumination being their only common characters. Some rarities form part of the more southern facet of this relict flora. Hutchinsia *(Hornungia petraea)* and Hoary Rockrose *(Helianthemum canum)* reach their northern location in the Dales, and are more favoured by the mild climate of Gower limestone sea cliffs, than the severe weather conditions of the northern Pennines. Several arctic plants reach their most southern British site in the Dales, Mountain Avens *(Dryas octapetala* plate 4b*)* high above Littondale or Alpine Bartsia (plate 10c) near Malham.

The Craven area of the Dales includes Malham and the Three Peaks and is formed of the Grear Scar Limestone. This rock is many hundred feet thick and was overtopped by younger layers of carboniferous limestone, the Yoredale Rocks. In several places the Yoreda Rocks are capped in Millstone Grit, and the summits of the Three Peaks are formed from this hard acid rock. In Wensleydale and to the north the Yoredale Rocks form the landscape, the Great Scar Limestone lying far down beneath. The layered strata of the Yoredale series forms the terraced scenery that is so familiar in Wensleydale and Wharfedale. Glaciation had a profound influence on the landscape. In several areas the glaciers scraped the soil off the blocks of the Great Scar Limestone and when the ice finally melted it left the bare white pavements that we know today (plate viii). Rainfall gradually dissolved the cementing material between the blocks form-

PLATE i
The River Tees at Low Force.

ing the deep, intricate passages we call grikes. The glaciers also left behind vast quantities of boulder clay scattered across the fells. In areas of impeded drainage these heavy soils became water-logged and peat development created blanket bogs. On freely-draining areas up to 610m the natural vegetation was woodland, Ash *(Fraxinus excelsior)* dominating over limestone soils. Forest clearance continued from neolithic times and the introduction of both rabbit and sheep to the uplands perpetuated the grazed grassland environment. From the 12th century the Cistercian monasteries of Fountains and Jervaux and the Augustinian Abbey at Bolton owned vast areas of the Dales. Great monastic sheep herds roamed the hillsides. Grasslands over limestone are rooted in shallow soils and undoubtedly in some places overgrazing led to soil erosion and appearance of the limestone pavement and grike. Fountains and Jervaux Abbeys are not on the Pennines proper but lie in the sheltered district just to the east over the fertile soils derived from magnesian limestone. This narrow band of rock stretches from near Nottingham to Darlington and is nowhere more than 6 miles wide. Far to the north-west, basalt from the Tertiary Volcanoes entered the area we now know as the Upper Tees Valley. The molten lava flowed into the carboniferous limestone of the fells and in very limited areas baked it white hot to form the crystalline sugar limestone. When solidified the basalt of the Whin Sill was resistant to water erosion and formed the spectacular waterfalls along the bed of the Tees (plate i).

The Yorkshire Dales National Park was designated in 1954 and covers 680 square miles. In the present book I do not restrict myself to its rigid boundary, but extend the area to the east to include Nidderdale along with the areas around Fountains and Jervaux and to the north to include Upper Teesdale.

The rare flowers of the Dales may be difficult to find, but the large majority of the limestone flowers are there for all to see, accessible by the hundreds of miles of public footpaths which cross and recross the hills. As with my two previous books on the Yorkshire Flora (Wild Flowers of the Wolds; Wild Flowers of the North York Moors National Park), the species mentioned are from my own personally collected records taken in the period 1976-1986. The wild flowers of the countryside are a priceless national heritage. They are an inheritance which must be treasured, but I believe they are a delight that must be shared. Only then will an overwhelming tide of public opinion demand their protection in future years.

WHARFEDALE

Wharfedale is an exceptional valley for the visiting botanist, offering a great range of habitats from the verdant river meadows to precipitous windswept crags high above the valley. These treeless heights have been a refuge for alpine flowers for thousands of years. In general the rich botanical areas lie to the north of Grassington coinciding with the appearance of the limestone country, and stretch to the hamlet of Cray at the beginning of the climb over to Wensleydale.

Walking through the river meadows from Grassington the eastern vista is dominated by a wooded hillside. A mixed woodland towers on limestone scars high above the wharfe, with trees stretching right down to the river bank. The scattered woodlands on the western bank serve to hide the extensive caravan sites which witness the popularity of this area as a summer holiday haunt. The eastern woodlands form Grass Wood and Bastow Wood. Grass Wood has been partly replanted and is an important reserve of the Yorkshire Wildlife Trust. The site is clearly primary woodland, for the range of woodland understory species is remarkable. Bastow Wood is a more natural woodland lying above Grass Wood, but has a very open canopy, is grazed and has a prevalence of grassland species.

Frequent understory plants in Grass Wood:-

Wood Cranesbill	*Geranium sylvaticum*
Woodruff	*Asperula odorata*
Mountain Melick	*Melica nutans*
Wood Sanicle	*Sanicula europaea*
Mountain Currant	*Ribes alpinum*
Herb Paris	*Paris quadrifolia*
Wood Sorrel	*Oxalis acetosella*
Dog's Mercury	*Mercurialis perennis*
Water Avens	*Geum rivale*

Lily of the Valley	*Convallaria majalis*
Columbine	*Aquilegia vulgaris*
Wood Anemone	*Anemone nemorosa*
Primrose	*Primula vulgaris*
Red Campion	*Silene dioica*
Bluebell	*Hyacinthoides non-scripta*
Wood Sage	*Teucrium scorodonia*
Early Purple Orchid	*Orchis mascula*

Open site species in Bastow Wood:-

Bird's Eye Primrose	*Primula farinosa*
Common Milkwort	*Polygala vulgaris*
Bitter Milkwort	*P. amara*
Small Scabious	*Scabiosa columbaria*
Vernal Sandwort	*Minuartia verna*
Mountain Everlasting	*Antennaria dioica*

Bastow Wood combines with Conistone Old Pasture to form a Site of Special Scientific Interest (S.S.S.I.) of national importance. In several areas of Grass Wood the limestone scars cause gaps in the tree canopy and sunshine streams down to the rock outcrops. This sunlit hillside blossoms into a herb-rich rock garden. The brilliant colours of the limestone flowers set against the green pasture and white scars of the valley below need only the blue sky of a summer's day to create a magical landscape; a place to pause and admire the natural beauty of this unique valley. The limestone at your feet is splashed with the white flowers of Burnet Rose *(Rosa pimpinellifolia)*, the startling pink of Bloody Cranesbill *(Geranium sanguineum* plate 7b*)*, the yellow of Rock Rose *(Helianthemum chamaecistus* plate 8c*)* and Horseshoe Vetch *(Hippocrepis comosa* plate 3b*)* and perfumed with Marjoram *(Origanum vulgare* plate 9b*)*, and Wild Thyme *(Thymus drucei* plate 6c*)*. Grass wood has numerous footpaths and although the wooded area is not large the rambler must set aside a good few hours to explore the hillside. Even after numerous visits to Grass Wood I always get lost in the maze of paths. I am fortunate that the photographer for this book usually accompanies me and is blessed with a much better sense of direction than I. I know these comments will strike a chord with most readers who have visited this Y.W.T. reserve.

Above Bastow Wood, the limestone pastures stretch to the sloping, white-cracked tableland of limestone pavement called Conistone Old Pasture. This pavement area lacks surface vegetation and appears a barren wilderness, until one peers into the shady recesses of the grikes which boast a rich display of limestone plants. For a small animal or insect the journey from the top of a pavement slab, down into a grike must represent the most dramatic climatic change inch for inch that can be experienced in British terrestrial habitats. Under the summer sun, the surface of the pavement is white hot, or swept by the restless wind, dazzling with reflected light. This brilliance is soon left behind as you travel down the chasm, where shade and accumulating vegetation create a cool humid corridor. It is not surprising that few plants cross the boundary between the two extremes and many species have a characteristic position, a depth zone in the grike.

Hart's Tongue Fern *(Phyllitis scolopendrium)* will usually be rooted on the bottom of the grike, growing where it can enjoy the moist still air. Wall Rue *(Asplenium ruta-muraria)* grows in tufts from under small ledges just beneath the surface of the pavement hiding from the full impact of the sun and wind. The tiny Three Fingered Saxifrage *(Saxifraga tridactylites)* roots in small areas of accumulated humus caught up in any shallow depressions on the surface of the pavement. Herb Robert *(Geranium robertianum)* is one of the few plants which often occupies several floors of the grike tower block. Throughout the country this small geranium is a common hedgerow flower, flourishing in the deep shade under the Hawthorn *(Crataegus monogyna)* canopy. Herb Robert has finely divided leaves which respond to changing light levels up and down the pavement by altering leaf pigmentation. Under the intense light of the limestone surface the leaves are predominantly red and as one traces the stems back into the shade of the grike the usual green chlorophyll pigments are re-instated.

The fern flora of the grike is the unique botanical feature of the pavements and any limestone pavement areas of reasonable size will reward the naturalist with the following species:-

Male Fern	*Dryopteris filix-mas*
Hart's Tongue Fern	*Phyllitis scolopendrium*

Lady Fern	*Athyrium filix-femina*
Broad Buckler Fern	*Dryopteris dilitata*
Hard Shield Fern	*Polystichum aculeatum*
Wall Rue	*Asplenium ruta-muraria*
Common Spleenwort	*A. trichomanes*
Brittle Bladder Fern	*Cystopteris fragilis*
Polypody	*Polypodium vulgare*
Bracken	*Pteridium aquilinum*

If you look carefully in crannies among the limestone rocks you will probably find the small fern, Green Spleenwort *(Asplenium viride)* which is restricted to calcareous rocks and can be differentiated from the Common Spleenwort quite easily. The latter has a black stem whereas that of Green Spleenwort is as green as the leaf-like frond. You may be fortunate and discover two rare ferns of the limestone. Holly Fern *(Polystichum lonchitis)* is primarily a mountain fern of basic rocks but does extend its range down the Pennine Chain to find suitable habitats in some limestone pavements. Limestone Polypody *(Thelypteris robertianum)* is found only on limestone rocks and screes but does not ascend above 610m (tree line) in the British Isles. Remembering that our alpine zone begins at this altitude we can see that this is not an alpine fern, but has one of its main distribution centres among the limestone rocks of the Yorkshire Dales.

The bare slabs of Conistone Pasture, shining white against the sky represent the extreme situation, the ultimate degradation and denudation of the upland limestone habitat. The Dales offer all the steps in the transition from the original dense primeval Ash *(Fraxinus excelsior)* woodland over vegetated pavement eg Grass Wood (although felling and replanting has changed the dominant trees) to areas where vegetation and soil have been eroded.

In spring the high pastures which stretch from Grassington to Conistone hold considerable interest for the naturalist. Despite the high grazing levels Mountain Pansy *(Viola lutea* plate 5b*)*, Wild Thyme *(Thymus drucei* plate 6c*)* and Thyme Leaved Speedwell *(Veronica serpyllifolia)* are frequently found beside the pathside. Mountain Everlasting *(Antennaria dioica* plate 2a*)* grows on the highest ridges. This is a member of the late glacial flora that is much more common on the mountain slopes in Scotland. Bitter Milkwort *(Polygala amara* figure 1*)* is another rarity of this short grassland.

FIGURE 1

A Common Milkwort
(Polygala vulgaris)

B Heath Milkwort
(Polygala serpyllifolia)

C Bitter Milkwort
(Polygala amara)

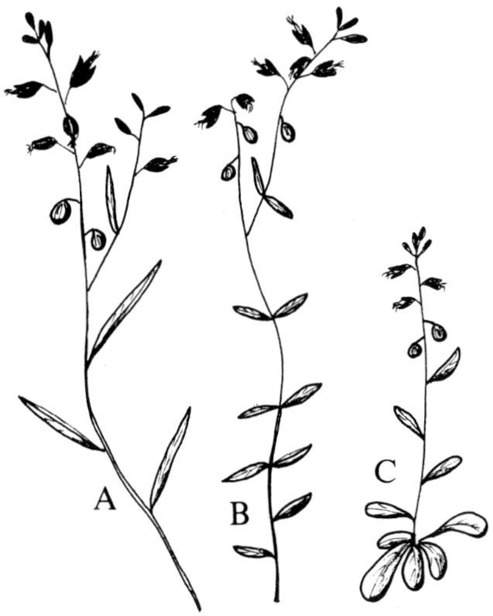

The three different milkworts of the Dales are easily distinguished on foliage shape and arrangement. Heath Milkwort *(Polygala serpyllifolia)* has many opposite stem leaves whereas Common Milkwort *(Polygala vulgaris)* has alternate stem leaves. Bitter Milkwort has a basal rosette of larger spoon-shaped leaves and then alternate stem leaves. The three plants are shown in Figure 1. Common Milkwort can be found in any limestone grassland and Heath Milkwort among Heather *(Calluna vulgaris)* and Bilberry *(Vaccinium myrtillus)* on freely draining acid soils over boulder clay. The Bitter Milkwort is of very limited distribution across the country as a whole, two of its distribution centres being Teesdale and the Craven Limestone.

The damper pastures in dips and depressions will display the beautiful pink flowers and tight mealy rosettes of Bird's Eye Primrose (plate 4c). Climbing down through limestone ravines near Conistone the cliffs carry Rockrose *(Helianthemum chamaecistus)* and Small Scabious *(Scabiosa columbaria)* in the spring, Marjoram *(Origanum vulgare)* and Orpine *(Sedum telephinum)* in mid-summer and the yellow heads of the Hawkweeds *(Hieracium sp.)* and Wall Lettuce *(Mycelis muralis)* in the shortening days of autumn. Here we have a range of cliff habitats which are high enough to discourage the voracious sheep.

Travelling towards Kettlewell scattered woodland lies on the slopes above the river and in ungrazed pockets, limestone outcrops show the Burnet Rose and Bloody Cranesbill; Bird's Eye Primrose occurs in the wet flushes between the rocks. Tributaries of the Wharfe flowing from Whernside pasture have interesting streamside pastures which have good populations of Fragrant Orchid *(Gymnadenia conopsea)* and Common Spotted Orchid *(Dactylorhiza fuchsii)*, and later in the summer these meadows are dotted white with Grass of Parnassus *(Parnassia palustris)*. Walking down from Providence Pot there is a clear transition from acid moorland vegetation on boulder clay tops to the calcareous pastures lower down the valley. Heather and Bracken *(Pteridium aquilinum)* dominate the upper moor with Harebell *(Campanula rotundifolia)* and Foxglove *(Digitalis purpurea* plate 2a*)* common among the rocks and the stream bed. Down past the limestone cliffs the bright green hue of the valley sides indicates the influence of the limestone and the change to a calcareous flora. The stream that follows this valley is called Dewbar Gill Beck and the slopes above the stream have been the site of lead mining activities. A spoil heap close by the water's edge shows the typical lead-tolerant plants:-

Spring Sandwort	*Minuartia verna*
Alpine Pennycress	*Thlaspi alpestre*
Common Sorrel	*Rumex acetosa*

Scattered plants of Mossy Saxifrage *(Saxifraga hypnoides* plate iv*)* are also present. Rejoining the main valley and continuing our journey north, good stretches of the river bank are provided with public footpaths. Butterbur *(Petasites hybridus)* is common along the river, the pink spike flower heads push through the ground in the early spring and are followed by the large rounded leaves that grow in size during the summer to dominate and outshade other riverside plants in their vicinity. In summer the river shingle will be brilliant with the red-splashed, yellow flowers of Monkey Flower *(Mimulus sp* plate 1a*)*. Usually the yellow petals have conspicuous deep-red blotches denoting the species *Mimulus luteus* which was introduced from Chile in the last century. More scattered markings are characteristic of *M. guttatus* which was introduced around the same time from North America. Both species have adapted well to the microclimate of British stream-sides and have escaped from gardens to become a common, naturalised flower in the British countryside. The wet meadows alongside the river have a rich potential flora and typical species include:-

Water Cress	*Nasturtium officinale*
Milkmaid	*Cardamine pratensis*
Water Avens	*Geum rivale*
Sweet Cicely	*Myrrhis odorata*
Lady's Mantle	*Alchemilla glabra agg.*
Large Bittercress	*Cardamine amara*
Alpine Scurvy Grass	*Cochlearia alpina*
Marsh Marigold	*Caltha palustris*
Common Bistort	*Polygonum bistorta*
Common Valerian	*Valeriana officinalis*
Brooklime	*Veronica beccabunga*
Common Spotted Orchid	*Dactylorhiza fuchsii*
Northern Marsh Orchid	*D. purpurella*

During a recent visit to the riverside, north of Buckden, I was disappointed to see that major works along the river, presumably for flood control, had disturbed several interesting areas. However flood control must be of vital importance to the farmers that live and work the riverside meadows, and it is worth remembering that without agricultural management the meadows and their flowers would not have life at all.

Hubberholme is at the top of Wharfedale and here the river flows out of Langstrothdale (plate xi). Climbing high above this delightful village the rambler will be rewarded with the best views of Wharfedale stretching away to the south. The steep slopes at the head of the dale are clothed with scattered grazed woodland, but even here one can find several typical woodland species.

Wild Garlic	*Allium ursinum*
Bluebell	*Hyacinthoides non-scripta*
Yellow Pimpernel	*Lysimachia nemorum*
Enchanter's Nightshade	*Circaea lutetiana*
Wood Cranesbill	*Geranium sylvaticum*
Woodruff	*Asperula odorata*
Early Purple Orchid	*Orchis mascula*

Above Hubberholme limestone crags are rather limited, but on the opposite valley side below Buckden Rake is a dramatic scar with ungrazed limestone cliffs.

The story of Wharfedale's flowers span the centuries from the ancient relict flora of the crags to the alien introductions of twentieth century travel. This is a unique valley that always rewards a return visit. There is certainly a new flower to find, a hidden ravine to explore, and a dramatic kaleidoscope of sky and cloud to watch as they chase across the green, limestone fells.

FACTS AND FICTION

Water Mint *(Mentha aquatica)*
This very aromatic herb has been used medicinally for many years, as an emetic, astringent and for treatment of diarrhoea. The leaves can be infused in water and taken to ease migraine headaches. The scent is certainly very pleasant, and coming from an important non-poisonous medicinal family, the *Labiatae*, is a plant to be recommended to the amateur herbalist.

Large Bittercress *(Cardamine amara)*
This plant can be differentiated from the common lilac Milkmaid by the white flowers with purple anthers. All the members of this genus taste like Water Cress *(Nasturtium officinale)* and give a rich source of Vitamin C when eaten raw in salads. The latin name of the genus comes from the belief that the plants were beneficial for those with a weak heart.

Common Sorrel *(Rumex acetosa)*
This is also an edible plant and was a popular vegetable in Tudor times. The sharp tang comes from the oxalic acid and it is the presence of this acid which gives Wood Sorrel *(Oxalis acetosella)* a similar name to the unrelated Common Sorrel. The leaves can be pulped into a green sauce to eat with fish. The plant may be harmful if eaten in large quantities. The wind pollinated flowers produce around 400 million pollen grains per individual.

WENSLEYDALE

Throughout the length of Wensleydale the River Ure grows and develops from its upland reaches near Hawes, through the well known waterfalls at Aysgarth to become the great river which curls and meanders south east from Wensley and flows wide and deep between the ancient streets of Ripon.

It is in these later stages of its progress that the Ure crosses the band of magnesian limestone which lies in a north-south strip in the lee of the Pennines. Over millenia this rock has weathered to form fertile soils on these rolling lowlands. Consequently the landscape yields good agricultural land and areas of natural wild vegetation are

PLATE ii
The River Swale above Keld.

sadly few. The wild flora of this limestone is particularly rich. Occupying warm habitats over light soils, the limestone favours northward migration of sun-loving southern plants eg. Squinancywort *(Asperula cynanchica* plate 12b*)* and Burnt Tip Orchid *(Orchis ustulata* plate 12a*)*. Even though natural areas are limited the botanist can examine ruins built from the local stone, and the quarries from whence the building material came. The river bank will also be a rewarding habitat to explore, together with any stretches of disused railway. West Tanfield has both these habitats close to the village centre. The springtime river bank of the Ure is a delight. Garden escapes such as Honesty *(Lunaria annua)* and Dame's Violet *(Hesperis matronalis)* compete for space with native vernal flowers. Butterbur *(Petasites hybridus)* heads make their appearance early in March, and as the days lengthen Water Chickweed *(Myosoton aquaticum)* and Water Figwort *(Scrophularia aquatica)* grow close to the turbulent river. You can also find Hemlock Water Dropwort *(Oenanthe crocata)* on this river bank. With umbel flower heads and profuse foliage growth this is a very poisonous plant which is much commoner in western districts of Britain.

Where the disused railway crosses the magnesian limestone there are fragments of line-bank grassland with a rich display of wild flowers. For example:-

Marjoram	*Origanum vulgare*
Dropwort	*Filipendula vulgaris*
Agrimony	*Agrimonia eupatoria*
Greater Knapweed	*Centaurea scabiosa*
Hairy St. John's Wort	*Hypericum hirsutum*
Kidney Vetch	*Anthyllis vulneraria*
Cowslip	*Primula veris*
Rest Harrow	*Ononis repens*
Salad Burnet	*Poterium sanguisorba*
Bladder Campion	*Silene vulgaris*

As you follow the river north towards the entrance of Wensleydale proper the Ure passes the famous Cistercian monastery of Jervaux Abbey, renowned by local naturalists for the variety of wild flowers growing on the ruins. There is usually a check list available for purchase at the entrance gate. Garden relicts survive from the gardens of the ancient monks and intermix with aliens of later introduction and also native wild flowers of the magnesian limestone

Examples of garden flowers:-

Aubretia	
Lilac	*Syringa*
Oregon Grape	*Mahonia*
Snapdragon	*Antirrhinum*

Examples of introductions to the area:-

Feverfew	*Chrysanthemum parthenium*
Ivy Leaved Toadflax	*Cymbalaria muralis*
Yellow Stonecrop	*Sedum acre*
Dark Mullein	*Verbascum nigrum*

Examples of the wild limestone flora of the area:-

Shining Cranesbill	*Geranium lucidum*
Viper's Bugloss	*Echium vulgare*
Musk Mallow	*Malva moschata*
Burnet Saxifrage	*Pimpinella saxifraga*

The river bank near Jervaux is well worth exploring. Here stately Bellflowers *(Campanula latifolia)* line the bank-side and associated wetland habitats have many interesting species. As an exercise in identification you can find four wet-site Willow Herbs growing together:-

Great Hairy Willow Herb	*Epilobium hirsutum*
Hoary Willow Herb	*E. parviflorum*
Bog Willow Herb	*E. palustre*
Short Fruited Willow Herb	*E. obscurum*

The different species of this family are always difficult to identify and perhaps better left to the enthusiast to puzzle over.

Other wet-site species include:-

Water Forget-me-not	*Myosotis scorpioides*
Branched Bur Reed	*Sparganium erectum*
Flag	*Iris pseudacorus*
Hard Rush	*Juncus inflexus*
Reed Mace	*Typha latifolia*
Reed Canary Grass	*Phalaris arundinaceae*
Water Speedwell	*Veronica anagallis-aquatica*
Yellow Rocket	*Barbarea vulgaris*
Marsh Hawksbeard	*Crepis paludosa*
Common Spotted Orchid	*Dactylorhiza fuchsii*

One stretch of pastureland along the river used to support a population of Burnt Tip Orchid (plate 12a) but on more recent visits to the area I have failed to find any blooms of this shy-flowering orchid. Areas of permanent pasture which remain free of fertiliser or herbicide are very limited. Fortunately near Wensley the Yorkshire Wildlife Trust has acquired such a field as a reserve. The Old Glebe Field has a rich flora, a valuable example of a habitat which used to be much more common in the past.

The Green Winged Orchid *(Orchis morio* plate 5a*)* still occurs in permanent pasture near Leyburn. Superficially similar to the Early Purple Orchid *(Orchis mascula* plate 12c*)*. This plant can be differentiated by its fewer flowers which have green veined sepals that form a partial hood at the apex of the flower. According to the European author, Sven Nilsson, this orchid was once much commoner in Europe than it is today. He suggested that 100 years ago the fields of southern Europe were often coloured purple-red with its blooms. Today it is common nowhere, a victim of the plough.

Leyburn stands at the head of Wensleydale and travelling west from the small village of Wensley one enters the heart of this broad beautiful valley. We have now left magnesian limestone behind and the valley shows the typical stepped sides of the Yoredale series. As one of the main east-west routes to the Lake District, and also a popular holiday area, the major road is usually busy with traffic. As always in the north of England it is easy to leave the crowds behind and to find quiet byways and shady lanes, free from cars. At this eastern end of the valley the naturalist will find it rewarding to climb from the riverside meadows towards Preston-under-Scar and visit the old limestone quarries above the village. From mid-June the drier areas of the quarry floor are alive with colour. Masses of Storksbill *(Erodium cicutarium* plate 11b*)* merge with three of the small wild cranesbills (Dove's Foot, *Geranium molle;* Small Flowered, *Geranium pusillum,* and Cut Leaved, *Geranium dissectum*) to create a cloud of brilliant pink which contrasts prettily with yellow carpets of Bird's Foot Trefoil *(Lotus corniculatus)* and Mouse Ear Hawkweed *(Hieracium pilosella).*

Other typical flowers to find include:-

Ox Eye Daisy	*Chrysanthemum leucanthemum*
Wild Strawberry	*Fragaria vesca*
Parsley Piert	*Aphanes arvensis*
Spring Whitlow Grass	*Erophila verna*
Rockrose	*Helianthemum chamaecistus*
Betony	*Betonica officinalis*
Yellow Stonecrop	*Sedum acre*
Cornsalad	*Valerianella locusta*
Felwort	*Gentianella amarella*

Silt washings from the light soils of the quarry accumulate in depressions to form impermeable soils. The extensive wet areas that result have a distinctive and interesting flora:-

Water Cress	*Nasturtium officinale*
Marsh Marigold	*Caltha palustris*
Brooklime	*Veronica beccabunga*
Marestail	*Hippuris vulgaris*
PondWeed	*Potomogeton sp.*
Lesser Spearwort	*Ranunculus flammula*

Growing close to the wettest areas you can find a fascinating, small and primitive fern, the Adder's Tongue *(Ophioglossum vulgare* Figure 2*)*, the sole survivor of a once extensive group of ferns. The Adder's Tongue is a living fossil, a tiny reminder of the ancient days when ferns dominated the landscape before the approaching dawn of the angiosperm day. Another fern with a similar history is the Moonwort *(Botrychium lunaria).* If you climb over to Swaledale from Preston, roadside verges have a good population of Moonwort

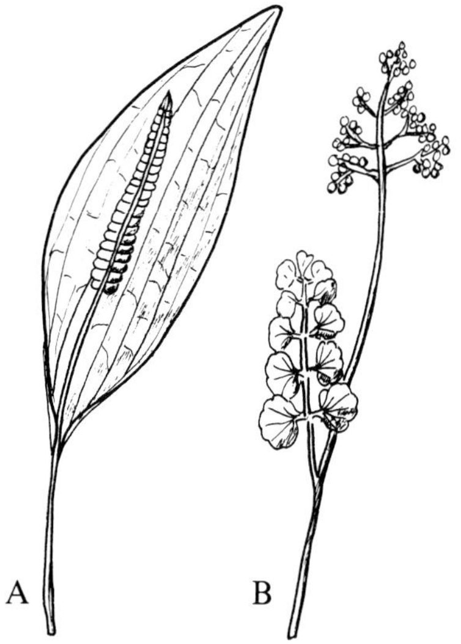

FIGURE 2

A Adder's Tongue Fern
(Ophioglossum vulgare)

B Moonwort
(Botrychium lunaria)

allowing a ready comparison of these two unusual ferns which are illustrated in Figure 2.

Many years ago I was advised to search for Herb Paris *(Paris quadrifolia* Plate 2c*)* in the woodlands near Preston, but after several visits I have failed to discover this elusive plant. Woodlands along the river near Aysgarth do indeed shelter this flower, along with many other flowers that are characteristic of calcareous woodland. This is a tangled forest. Dense, deep thickets of tree and shrub alternate with more open tracts where sunshine streams through the sparse branches to illuminate the woodland floor.

Dog's Mercury	*Mercurialis perennis*
Bluebell	*Hyacinthoides non-scripta*
Pignut	*Conopodium majus*
Goldilocks	*Ranunculus auricomus*
Wood Cranesbill	*Geranium sylvaticum*
Wood Melick	*Melica uniflora*
Early Purple Orchid	*Orchis mascula*
Wood Speedwell	*Veronica montana*
Wild Garlic	*Allium ursinum*
Bugle	*Ajuga reptans*
Toothwort	*Lathraea squamaria*
Ground Ivy	*Glechoma hederacea*

The trees of the woodland are a mixture of species, Oak *(Quercus robur)*, Ash *(Fraxinus excelsior)* and Hazel *(Corylus avellana)* being the most common. Near Aysgarth the pathways through the woodland are often a quagmire of mud, the result of running close to the river torrent and being puddled by the feet of numerous holidaymakers who visit the famous waterfalls. Drier paths lead along the Hazel woodland on the scarp above the valley. This stand has classic evidence of coppice management and is almost pure Hazel, with a poorly developed understory.

From the splashing brooks, high on the hillside to the rushing river of the valley plain, the water-side flora of Wensleydale is perhaps the most exciting and unique feature of the naturalist's Wensleydale. Before the pure waters of the hillside tumble towards the broad heterogeneous river they can traverse habitats which vary from shallow meadows to rocky ravines. In the early summer streamside meadows near Aysgarth are covered in Sea Thrift *(Armeria maritima* Plate 3a*)* and Alpine Scurvy Grass *(Cochlearia alpina)* and later into the summer their blooms are replaced by the delicate fragile flowers of Grass of Parnassus *(Parnassia palustris)*. Following this stream up the hillside one can find Bird's Eye Primrose *(Primula farinosa* plate 4c*)*, Marsh Valerian *(Valeriana dioica)* and Butterwort *(Pinguicula vulgaris)* growing together in the wet meadow. Streams flowing into Semerwater have a similar waterside flora sheltering in a steep, green valley whose slopes are yellow with Globeflowers *(Trollius europaeus,* front cover*)* and dotted with Early Purple Orchid *(Orchis mascula* plate 12c). Above Askrigg, water cascades down waterfalls and through rocky, wooded slopes. Here streamside splash areas are covered in Opposite Leaved Golden Saxifrage *(Chrysosplenium oppositifolium)* and on wet, sheltered, but deeper soils stands of Water Chickweed *(Mysoton aquaticum)* carpet the narrow floor of the ravine.

South of Bainbridge the short course of the river Bain brings water into the Ure from the 40 hectare expanse of Semerwater, one of Yorkshire's only three natural bodies of water. Escape of lake water is hindered by a terminal moraine through which the outflow passes down a steep-sided valley. The name Semerwater is thought to have evolved from the words "sea" and "mere" perhaps reflecting the rapid and large fluctuations of water level that occur during periods of heavy rainfall. Marsh vegetation is particularly well developed at the south edge of the lake, where typical vegetation includes:-

Bog Bean	*Menyanthes trifoliata*
Marsh Ragwort	*Senecio aquaticus*
Common Spotted Orchid	*Dactylorhiza fuchsii*
Marsh Cinquefoil	*Potentilla palustris*
Yellow Water Lily	*Nuphar lutea*
Bottle Sedge	*Carex rostrata*

In Wensleydale one is never far from the hand of man, even in the remote environs of Semerwater. Caraway *(Carum carvi* plate 2b*)* is an escape from cultivation which is naturalised by a village streamside above this lake. The seeds of this attractive umbellifer are used in baking (Caraway seed cake) and although it is a native plant it is very rarely found except as a relict of cultivation.

FACTS AND FICTION

Thrift *(Armeria maritima* plate 3a*)*
These delightful pink flowers have been cultivated in rock gardens for four centuries, and are recommended for gardeners trying to attract butterflies. A clump of thrift was pictured on the reverse side of the George VI old brass three pence bit. Geographical isolation of inland colonies has resulted in the evolution of different forms. The length of the flower head stalk is particularly characteristic. Plants on Widdybank Fell Teesdale have longer stalks than those found on Pennine mine sites.

Herb Paris *(Paris quadrifolia* Plate 2c*)*
As would be expected from the Latin name, most plants have four leaves in a whorl, but specimens with 3-8 can be found. The plant is poisonous and has a slightly obnoxious smell. The aroma attracts carrion flies as pollinators. This rather rare plant is restricted to primary woodlands almost always over calcareous soils.

Ground Ivy *(Glechoma hederacea* Figure 3*)*
This is an ancient medicinal plant which has been used for ailments as diverse as wounds and worms. Before hops were introduced into Britain, Ground Ivy was added to ale during brewing. The dried or fresh leaves can also be used as a seasoning.

TEESDALE

My first introduction to the flowers of the Yorkshire Dales was through a research project on the climate and vegetation of the Upper Tees Valley. Since that time I have taken many adult education groups along this vale looking for wild flowers. I regard the botanical interest of the Tees valley from Middleton to Cow Green so highly that it is the only weekend field trip that I have repeated several times over the past ten years. I am not simply referring to the famous fells at the top of the valley, but also to the beautiful scenery and flowers along this twelve mile stretch of the river. The northern border of Yorkshire follows the Tees, but I propose to ignore this man-made unnatural boundary, and discuss thc entire valley of the Upper Tees. The Spring Gentian *(Gentiana verna* plate 3c*)* is undoubtedly the most famous flower of the valley. No-one who has seen clusters of Gentians brilliant blue against the grass, would question their right to be the emblem of Teesdale. On a sunny day in May, the casual rambler may be fortunate and pass the Gentian pen on Widdybank Fell when the flowers are open to the sky and a breathtaking blue. Let's be realistic and point out the several factors which combine to make this a lucky chance. The flower of any one plant is only open for about a week and with the vagaries of our British springtime weather, flowering time at any particular site can vary over a four-week period. The flower of the Gentian is also shy of opening when the weather is cold or overcast. I have usually visited the valley during the Spring Bank Holiday and this upland climate has given weather varying from still-blue skies under a scorching sun to gale-force icy winds blowing horizontal sleet. In spite of these difficulties we have always been able to find Gentians in full bloom. The clue to the puzzle lies in the several sites where one can find these flowers, all beside the public footpaths. Some Gentians grow close by the Alston road whilst others grow on Cronkley Fell some 164 metres above. During any one springtime the lower altitude populations will flower a week or two before the high

PLATE iii
The Churchyard, Horton-in-Ribblesdale, with
Ox Eye Daisy *(Chrysanthemum leucanthemum)*.

windswept plants on the fells. If the spring is early we look first on Cronkley Fell, if late we look along the road or near the river banks.

Teesdale has much to offer aside from the rare Gentians. The landscape is very different from the other long Dales to the south. This shallow, wide valley is dotted with the white-washed farms which form part of Lord Barnard's Raby Estate. The Tees rises on the slopes of Cross Fell and used to flow gently across weathered, sedimentary rocks until it reached the hard rocks of the Whin Sill at Cauldron Snout. The columnar basalt of the Whin Sill forms the bed of the spectacular waterfalls in the upper reaches of the Tees, Cauldron Snout, High Force and Low Force (Plate i). The flat plain of Cow Green narrowed sharply to the approaches of Cauldron Snout and created the obvious and only place for a reservoir in the Upper Tees Valley.

In Teesdale we have flowers which are a mirror of the past, survivors from that period of time when melting ice gave way to a low, herbaceous arctic vegetation, with flowers of every colour and form: not just individual species as we have perhaps in Wharfedale or high on the crags of Ingleborough, but whole, intact communities of flowers which have grown together, flowered together, set seed and been reborn together for 8,000 years. Our present understanding of how our vegetation has changed in successive millenia began with the discovery of such relict populations. They are irreplaceable fragments and as such are priceless. How could the government of the day allow a 300 hectare reservoir to encroach on this unique environment, destroy 10% of the sugar limestone habitats outright, change drainage and erosion patterns for all time and cause unpredictable changes in this relict ecosystem?

Hindsight is a lazy vision but successive generations will condemn in amazement the desecration of this natural area which is arguably the most important botanical site in England. During the economic boom of the 1960's industries at the mouth of the Tees demanded a regular water supply down the river, a minimum flow that was independent of the season. This requirement necessitated a header reservoir which could supplement summer rainfall inflow. When the reservoir was approved these industries provided money for many research projects on every aspect of the natural history of Upper Teesdale from invertebrates to pollen analysis. Some of this money paid my salary during the four year research fellowship which facilitated my return to England after studying in the U.S.A. This fact did not blind me to the enormity of the crime of Cow Green. Let us leave the recent activities of man and follow the fascinating story of the Teesdale flowers.

At the end of the last Ice Age, the ice and snow melted as the climate became milder. An arctic-alpine vegetation swept north across England in the wake of the Ice. This low-growing community of herb, grasses and sedges reached Upper Teesdale and flourished in full sunshine on the windswept fells. The vegetation thrived on the limestone soils and also colonised the unique sugar limestone outcrops which occur on the tops of Widdybank and Cronkley Fells. This sugar limestone had been formed when the molten basalt lava of the Whin Sill flowed across the landscape baking parts of the carboniferous limestone to create a crumbly crystalline rock, now called sugar limestone.

As the climate gradually became warmer coniferous trees invaded the valleys and fells. The technicolour alpine turf was cast into a perpetual shade from which it could not escape. Across most of England the tiny colourful herbs disappeared for ever, and the landscape was covered first in conifers and then in broadleaved woodland. In Teesdale the crumbling, rotting soils of the sugar limestone were not favourable for tree seedlings. The woodland could not gain ascendancy over these fells. The Teesdale rarities survived in full sunshine on this rock during the period of maximum forest cover. By 1,000 BC man had begun forest clearance and gradually the uplands emerged from their forest cloister into the wide open sky. From now on the post-glacial floral relicts could extend their range and spread as clouds of colour across the hillsides onto the normal limestone soils. The Teesdale rarities are not all arctic or alpine flowers; their common denominator is their need for full sunshine and intolerance of forest shade. Thus we can find Hoary Rockrose *(Helianthemum canum)* a continental plant that reaches its northern limit in Britain on Cronkley Fell. Its long isolation from nearest populations on North and South Wales coastal cliffs has resulted in slight genetic changes and it is now recognised as a separate variety. The Teesdale Gentian itself has an unusual geographical range, and although it occurs in mountains of mainland Europe, the only other site in the British Isles is to the west on the Burren in Co. Clare, Ireland. Many other Teesdale rarities are more common in Scotland and are reaching the southern limits of their range when growing in Teesdale eg. Mountain Avens *(Dryas octapetala* plate 4b) and Alpine Bartsia *(Bartsia alpina* plate 10c). We begin our look at the Tees at the most depressing place in the Upper Valley. The car park at Cow Green leads on to the tarmac road over Widdybank Fell and on to the dam itself, where one can pause and admire man's achievements in concrete and clay! The calcareous streams on this fell are probably the most fragile of Teesdale habitats, and are the site of the rarest plant in the area, namely Bog Sandwort *(Minuartia stricta)*. This is its only site in Britain. Since many visitors walk across Widdybank Fell these streams must be protected and access is restricted to the tarmac path. The rarer waterside plants cannot be seen from the path and the amateur naturalist must rest content to examine the drier habitats over the sugar limestone, or the old pit shafts along the way.

Lesser Club Moss	*Selaginella selaginoides*
Moonwort	*Botrychium lunaria*
Spring Sandwort	*Minuartia verna*
Spring Gentian	*Gentiana verna*
Spring Sedge	*Carex caryophyllea*

At Cauldron Snout we join a branch of the Pennine Way which takes us down beside the waterfall to walk under the basalt cliffs of Falcon Clints. Boulders and debris litter the hillside, but among them we can find several interesting ferns.

Parsley Fern	*Cryptogramma crispa*
Fir Club Moss	*Lycopodium selago*
Black Spleenwort	*Asplenium adiantum-nigrum*
Broad Buckler Fern	*Dryopteris dilitata*

High on the cliffs themselves, look for a small delicate fern, the Green Spleenwort *(Asplenium viride)* about 7.5 cm long. This fern favours limestone rocks and is evidence of calcareous seepage from the limestones of Widdybank Fell above. Bird's Eye Primrose *(Primula farinosa* plate 4c) grows on these same, wet cliff ledges. From this point this small and beautiful, pink primrose can be found intermittently on the river bank all the way down to Middleton. Looking across the river we get our first glimpse of Shrubby Cinquefoil *(Potentilla fruticosa)* and in June the opposite bank is a yellow shrubbery of this rare plant which produces a profusion of five-petalled flowers. The long flowering season of this small shrub has encouraged nurserymen to culture several horticultural varieties which are sold as hedging plants. If you find them expensive for this purpose they will make an interesting specimen shrub in any garden. In July on this same river bank under Cronkley Scar the yellow shrubs are joined by more orange-yellow mats of Yellow Mountain Saxifrage *(Saxifraga aizoides* plate 7c*)*. This plant is common across wet mountain tracks in Scotland, whether the rock be acid or calcareous. Although the flower is not rare in the Yorkshire Dales it usually hugs the limestone flushes or streamside crags. Two common small trees of the river bank are Tea-Leaved Willow *(Salix phyllicifolia* plate 4a*)* and Bird Cherry *(Prunus padus* plate 6b*)*. The catkins of the willow shine attractively in the May sunshine, but the blossoms of the Bird Cherry are a riot of frothy white racemes which often cover the whole tree.

As you travel down the valley the wet riverside pastures of both the Tees and the Langdon Beck now boast many of the rarities which were once restricted to the sugar limestone outcrops and the sykes that cut through them.

Alpine Bartsia	*Bartsia alpina*
Alpine Bistort	*Polygonum viviparum*
Broad Leaved Cotton Grass	*Eriophorum latifolium*
Spring Gentian	*Gentiana verna*

Away from the river the pastures are still very rich in wild flowers and a delight to explore in the early spring.

Marsh Valerian	*Valeriana dioica*
Bog Violet	*Viola palustris*
Milkmaid	*Cardamine pratensis*
Bog Stitchwort	*Stellaria alsine*
Ragged Robin	*Lychnis flos-cuculi*
Common Spotted Orchid	*Dactylorhiza fuchsii*
Early Marsh Orchid	*D. incarnata*
Northern Marsh Orchid	*D. purpurella*

These meadows also contain several springtime herbs which are more familiar in the woodland environment. Their presence being evidence that this area was once wooded.

Examples of these woodland herbs:-

Early Purple Orchid	*Orchis mascula*
Wood Anemone	*Anemone nemorosa*
Wood Sorrel	*Oxalis acetosella*

In the longer, hotter days of full summer these same meadows flaunt Grass of Parnassus *(Parnassia palustris)* and Fragrant Orchid *(Gymnadenia conopsea)*, often massed together in the grass. The bridge across the river near Cronkley Farm gives access from the road to public footpaths which cross over Cronkley Fell. An easy short climb is rewarded by breathtaking views to Cross Fell, Dufton Fell, and close below the rugged cliffs of Falcon Clints that have just been described. It is on Cronkley Fell that we find the second major outcrop of sugar limestone. Here the plateau hilltop is devoid of calcareous streams and the alpine vegetation is that of dry sites. The distance over the river to Widdybank Fell is less than a mile, but we find quite differing communities of flowers:-

Mountain Avens	*Dryas octapetala*
Rockrose	*Helianthemum chamacistus*
Hoary Rockrose	*H. canum*
Twisted Whitlow Grass	*Draba incana*
Hair Sedge	*Carex capillaris*
Teesdale Violet	*Viola rupestris*

These flowers are joined by those listed as dry-site species of Widdybank Fell. Mountain Avens and Hoary Rockrose carpet the rocks in one of the Gentian pens. Mountain Avens will be familiar to naturalists who have climbed calcareous mountains in Scotland, or have been lucky enough to visit the Arctic. The beautiful white flowers (plate 4b) are fully 2.5cm across and hold a yellow frothy centre of numerous stamens. Coupled with evergreen, crinkly leaves the whole plant is both extremely attractive and easy to recognise, also difficult to miss when it flowers in June. Here on Cronkley, you can find the small elusive Teesdale Violet *(Viola rupestris)*, but you should time your visit for mid May. The Gentians will not be in bloom but you may be rewarded by finding the small lilac violet that has finely hairy-leaf stalks and fruits, along with leaves which roll at their edges. This is a difficult violet to correctly identify, and I speak from experience. Although we call it Teesdale Violet it is not uncommon on rocky hillsides in the Alps, the habitat aptly reflecting its specific name *rupestris* (of rocks). Search closely in the close cropped grass for the tiny, primitive ferns and sedges that grow on Cronkley, often found between the starry flowers of the Spring Sandwort *(Minuartia verna)*. Below Cronkley farm the Tees cuts a channel between steep hillsides which are clothed in scattered Juniper *(Juniperus communis)*. Juniper once covered large areas of the Upper Tees Valley. Clearing and grazing has depleted the woodland to its present patchy occurrence. Juniper berries were traditionally used to smoke fish, and the Tees below High Force was an important salmon river.

Before the reservoir was built at Cow Green, the great Tees flowed powerful and strong in wet seasons, compared with its gentle presence in dry. The riverside rocks and shingle were sometimes caught in the swirl and destruction of the river in spate, and at other times held dry above the water, a perfect seed bed for propagules carried down by the river in its angry mood. The waters-edge of rivers which rise in the upland zone and flow through the lowlands is a classic place for discovering alpine rarities at low altitudes. Thus it was with the Tees: Mountain Everlasting *(Antennaria dioica* plate 2a*)* and Alpine Bistort *(Polygonum viviparum)* can still be found near Low Force (plate i), nestling in the riverside rocks. Now the reservoir regulates the flow of the river, and the river in spate is a much rarer phenomenon. We were fortunate enough to visit Teesdale in 1986 over a weekend of torrential rain and gale force winds. I would not have felt so fortunate had the rain not fallen solely during the night and cleared to brilliant, windy days with white clouds flying across blue, sunlit skies. Water was flowing over the dam and during this weekend we saw waterfalls in dramatic spate, and the river high along the banks.

The woodlands near Low Force have many of the common woodland herbs that are associated with areas that have been continuously wooded. Wild Garlic *(Allium ursinum)*, Goldilocks *(Ranunculus auricomus)* and Bluebell *(Hyacinthoides non-scripta)* are particularly common near Wynch Bridge. In May the blue-purple flowers of Ground Ivy *(Glechoma hederacea)* and Bugle *(Ajuga reptans)* are frequent at the woodland edge. Many people have difficulty in distinguishing between these and Self Heal *(Prunella vulgaris)*, which does not usually flower until well into June. They are all members of

FIGURE 3

A Ground Ivy
(Glechoma hederacea)

B Bugle
(Ajuga reptans)

C Self Heal
(Prunella vulgaris)

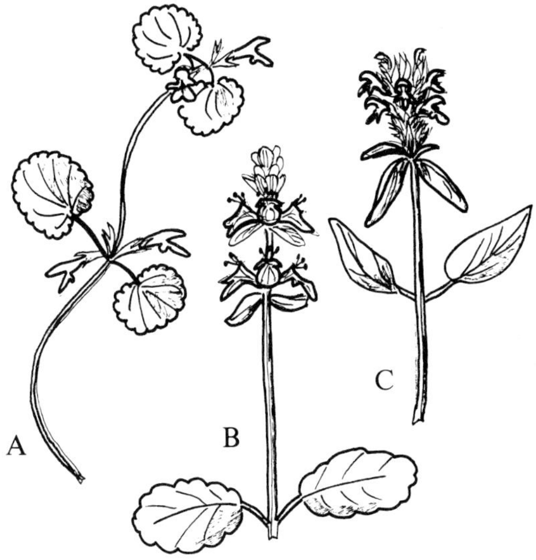

the mint family and can be separated on flower shape and foliage characters (figure 3).

The hay meadows between Low Force and Newbiggin are probably the most spectacular in the Dales. Over the centuries the Raby Estate has controlled the farming practices of tenant farmers; these policies have favoured the wild meadow flowers. June is the time to see the meadows at their best, a profusion of pink and white blossoms in the restless breeze, over a backcloth of yellow buttercups and rattles.

The pink flowers:

Red Clover	*Trifolium pratense*
Wood Cranesbill	*Geranium sylvaticum*
Water Avens	*Geum rivale*

The white flowers:

Meadow Saxifrage	*Saxifraga granulata*
Pignut	*Conopodium majus*
Sweet Cicely	*Myrrhis odorata*

Close to the river bank the Globe Flowers *(Trollius europaeus,* front cover*)* hold the attention massed in the corners of the meadow or clinging to the rocky slopes above the river. The lemon orb of the Globe Flower appears early in the spring, a yellow haze of the lower meadows when the Gentians are at their most beautiful in the upper grasslands. By mid July the hay meadows have been cut, but in hidden corners and by stream banks the pink and white theme continues with the flowering of the late season perennials.

White:

Angelica	*Angelica sylvestris*
Meadow Sweet	*Filipendula ulmaria*
Ox Eye Daisy	*Chrysanthemum leucanthemum*

Pink:

Hard Heads	*Centaurea nigra*
Greater Burnet	*Sanguisorba officinale*
Melancholy Thistle	*Cirsium heterophyllum*
Marsh Thistle	*C. palustre*

The Tees valley between Middleton and Cow Green is quite unique. Footpaths stretch along this whole length of river and give access to varied habitats, changing landscapes and the most exciting display of wild flowers in the Dales.

FACTS AND FICTION

Melancholy Thistle *(Cirsium heterophyllum* plate vi*).*
The solitary head was thought to have a sad appearance, and from the Doctrine of Signatures the plant was used in the Middle Ages to cure melancholy. It was thought especially effective when the leaves were steeped in wine!! The thistle was first recorded in England by Thomas Penny who was born in Cambridge in 1530. A cleric by profession he had a great interest in botany and recorded wild flowers in many parts of Europe.

Juniper *(Juniperus communis).*
This evergreen conifer was one of the first trees to return to Britain after the last Ice Age. The aromatic berries take two years to ripen to the purple bloom, when they can be used to flavour gin. This shrub was once more common, and in the Dales is perhaps best seen around and above High Force.

Water Avens *(Geum rivale).*
The word "avens" means healing and this is an old medicinal plant which was once used to cure the plague. The flower easily crosses with the woodland relative Wood Avens *(Geum urbanum)* and the resultant hybrids are often larger than the parents and delicate mixtures of pink and yellow. The purple coloured roots of Water Avens have been dried and used as a substitute for cocoa.

SWALEDALE

Swaledale is a quiet valley, beloved by walker rather than motorist. The road above Reeth is narrow and winding, taking the traveller into the heart of the riverside hay meadows. For myself the fascination of this Dale lies in the contrast between these peaceful waterside pastures and the restless hillsides above the head of the valley, where landscape and sky often meet in a violent union. At heights above 550m, at the very watershed of the Pennines we can find a steep ravine where time has stood still for centuries: of little interest to the hill farmer, or even the walker who usually favours the windswept tops for their views west to the Lake District across the Vale of Eden; little touched by the business of man and known only to the hillside ewe who may explore the streamside pasture in search of virgin grass. The Ring Ousel has known this crag for generation after generation; flying down the ravine its call echoes between opposing cliffs. The steep rocks tower above the narrow stream-bed which suddenly drops dramatically in a foaming waterfall. This is a harsh environment, inhospitable to the sturdy Oak or elegant Ash. Even those intrepid mountaineers, the beautiful Rowan and slender Birch, only occur as occasional, stunted silhouettes against the rugged hillside and the Pennine sky. True the British climate always seeks to surprise, but never more so than at this peak of the northern hills where I have sunbathed on streamside rocks at Easter and battled through driving rain in gale-force fog in June, although to the weather watcher the latter may seem a contradiction.

Outlined is an upland environment of rock, scree and stream, set under our fickle upland climate, defined is a perfect habitat for the persistence of the late glacial arctic-alpine flora which returned to Britain in the wake of the melting ice some 10,000 years ago.

This is a precipitous valley where some alpines have colonised bare stony slopes and others have dipped their roots into the crystal brook, nestling hidden from the sheep by waterside boulders; a quiet lonely place, vibrant with the echoes of a past that is the present,

PLATE iv
Mossy Saxifrage *(Saxifrage hypnoides).*

where the pages of the volume on British botanical history are the flowering boulders bound securely in the protective cover of two steep valley sides.

Some of the interesting alpines I have found here are:-

Alpine Scurvy Grass	*Cochlearia alpina*
Twisted Whitlow Grass	*Draba incana*
Yellow Mountain Saxifrage	*Saxifraga aizoides*
Alpine Bistort	*Polygonum viviparum*
Mossy Saxifrage	*Saxifraga hypnoides*

Twisted Whitlow Grass *(Draba incana)* is not a grass, but a small white cabbage and the twisted epithet refers to a turn in the pod-like fruit *(Silicula).* The delicate stalks hold a cluster of small flowers and rise from an attractive deep-green rosette of slightly toothed leaves. This is a plant of dry places, which cannot compete with vigorous grassland plants, preferring to struggle for root-hold on crumbling scree or rocky slab rather than jostle for living space in the easier habitat near the stream.

It is by the stream that you will find another white member of this same family *(cruciferae)*. Alpine Scurvy Grass *(Cochlearia alpina)* is a dwarf form of the Common Scurvy Grass *(C. officinalis)* which is such a familiar flower around our coastline in May. The rounded leaves are quite succulent and the plant often produces profuse foliage in suitable sheltered habitats. The upland summer is often very short, barely time for plants to flower and set their seed. The Alpine Bistort *(Polygonum viviparum)* can avoid this problem by producing tiny bulbils as well as flowers. These ripen quickly and the plant is thus able to reproduce vegetatively even if the summer is too brief for true seed set. The white flowers of Mossy Saxifrage *(Saxifraga hypnoides* plate iv*)* grow in profusion by the stream, but we cannot truly call this pretty plant an alpine since it occurs south into Derbyshire where it has the local name Dovedale Moss.

This steep valley is not just a home for tiny rock plants. Two of our pink native cranesbills grow on the cliffs. The large, showy Wood Cranesbill *(Geranium sylvaticum* Figure 4*)* and the smaller (less than 1.25cm) Shining Cranesbill *(G.lucidum)*. The rounded shiny leaves of the latter give its name and also allow easy recognition. As the valley widens downslope, wet marshland by the stream is a home for Marsh Valerian *(Valeriana dioica)* and Bird's Eye Primrose *(Primula farinosa* plate 4c*)* along with insectivorous Butterwort *(Pinguicula vulgaris)*. The dry limestone grassland on the summit of Tailbridge Hill is very reminiscent of such sites in Teesdale. Although the Teesdale rarities are absent, the Blue Mountain Grass *(Sesleria caerulea)* swards are species rich, if somewhat overgrazed.

Rockrose	*Helianthemum chamaecistus*
Hairy Rock Cress	*Arabis hirsuta*
Spring Whitlow Grass	*Erophila verna*
Mountain Pansy	*Viola lutea*
Fairy Flax	*Linum catharticum*
Salad Burnet	*Poterium sanguisorba*
Spring Sedge	*Carex caryophyllea*

As one descends eastwards from these windy heights, one enters Swaledale proper and soon reaches the riverside at Keld (plate ii). The hay meadows here are remarkable for their profusion and variety of wild flowers. In late June the meadows are purple and white with Wood Cranesbill and Pignut *(Conopodium majus)*; clustered in patches among the grass are the pink spikes of Common Bistort *(Polygonum bistorta)* and on wetter sites the pink-red bells of Water Avens *(Geum rivale)*. Bistort is a far cry from the garden weed Red Leg *(Polygonum persicaria)* to which it is closely related. The attractive features of Bistort have been recognised by gardeners and a cultivar is now a frequent member of the herbaceous border where the long pink flower heads have an extended flowering season. The walk along the river bank from Keld to Muker provides a mosaic of differing habitats: limestone woodland, lead spoil heap, dry limestone grassland, wet marshland, hay meadow and riverside shingle. During the summer all these fragments will show their own characteristic flowers; from the diminutive Moonwort *(Botrychium lunaria* Figure 2*)* on the old spoil to the stately Bell Flower *(Campanula latifolia)* near Kisdon Force. During an easy walk along the riverside paths in June I recorded over 170 different flowering plants and ferns.

Above all it is the hay meadows which attract the naturalist's attention. Sadly over the years these 'natural' meadows have become depleted in number. Some have been 'improved' with use of fertiliser and herbicide, others have been ploughed and reseeded with Rye Grass *(Lolium perenne)*. A recent and damaging tendency is of cutting for silage, where meadow vegetation is cropped before the early summer flowers have set seed and completed their life cycle. These meadows have evolved with the traditional farming practice of cutting for hay in mid July. The silage meadow will quickly become devoid of the rarer flowers, their natural beauty lost forever. Fortunately one meadow near Muker is protected under the management of the Yorkshire Wildlife Trust as Yellands Meadow Reserve.

In a typical Swaledale hay meadow you may find these herbs:-

Pignut	*Conopodium majus*
Sweet Cicely	*Myrrhis odorata*
Yellow Rattle	*Rhinanthus minor*
Common Bistort	*Polygonum bistorta*
Wood Cranesbill	*Geranium sylvaticum*
Milkmaid	*Cardamine pratensis*
Hard Heads	*Centaurea nigra*

Meadow Buttercup	*Ranunculus acris*
Bulbous Buttercup	*R. bulbosus*
Dandelion	*Taraxacum officinale*
Common Sorrel	*Rumex acetosa*
Rough Hawkbit	*Leontodon hispidus*
Bugle	*Ajuga reptans*
Melancholy Thistle	*Cirsium heterophyllum*

Melancholy Thistle is a strange emotive name for a thistle, perhaps because the flower head is always borne single on a long stalk (plate vi). This very attractive thistle is found in English northern uplands and then commonly in Scotland; it has long narrow leaves which are hardly prickly but have white backs to the leaf blade.

The wettest parts of the meadow have a distinctive mixture of flowers, a good place for discovering the variety of forms of the spotted and marsh orchids (plate 5c). These orchids will be numerous in the meadows of late June. Other characteristic species include:-

Marsh Bedstraw	*Galium palustre*
Marsh Ragwort	*Senecio aquaticus*
Ragged Robin	*Lychnis flos-cuculi*
Bog Stitchwort	*Stellaria alsine*
Marsh Valerian	*Valeriana dioica*
Common Spotted Orchid	*Dactylorhiza fuchsii*
Early Marsh Orchid	*D. incarnata*
Northern Marsh Orchid	*D. purpurella*

Marsh Ragwort *(Senecio aquaticus)* is more attractive than its noxious relative, Common Ragwort *(S. jacobea)*. Although the flowers are of the same yellow hue, Marsh Ragwort has reddish stems that bear broader leaves overtopped by larger flower heads which are lax and not arranged in a flat-topped cluster, as is seen in Common Ragwort.

Swaledale has a peaceful landscape, less affected than the other Yorkshire Dales by the hustle and bustle of twentieth-century life, retaining time honoured methods of farming and providing rich rewards for the naturalist. I hope that modern methods of farming are not allowed to spoil the marvellous, irreplaceable heritage of the Swaledale hay meadow.

FACTS AND FICTION

Common Bistort *(Polygonum bistorta)*.
This plant is the main ingredient of ledger pudding, made from a country recipe of wild plants and hard boiled egg. This pudding was traditionally eaten in the Dales at Easter. The root has been used medicinally to stop internal bleeding.

Ragged Robin *(Lychnis flos-cuculi)*.
The dissected petals on the flower were likened to the torn, red uniform coat of a soldier expelled from the ranks for cowardice; this comparison gave the plant the specific epithet *flos-cuculi*. This delightful flower of wet meadows can make the marsh turn bright pink. Unlike the Red Campion *(Silene dioica)* both sexes are present in a single flower which fruits readily in late June.

Dandelion *(Taraxacum officinale)*.
The common name comes from the French for lion's teeth and refers to the shape of the leaf segments. The leaf is a rich source of minerals and can be eaten both raw and cooked. The plant has a milky juice which stimulates the kidney and urination. The dried root can be used as a substitute for coffee. Why not try a raw Dandelion sandwich with a dash of Worcester sauce!

NIDDERDALE

When one reflects on the old boundaries of Yorkshire, the county line enclosed a vast country with a very varied geology and scenery. It is perhaps surprising that despite its size it boasted only four natural bodies of water, two of these being in the Yorkshire Dales, namely Malham Tarn and Semerwater. The absence of lakes or reservoirs in porous limestone country is to be expected, but larger bodies of water set in verdant valleys have always delighted man's eye. Thus it is refreshing to drive north from Pateley Bridge into Nidderdale and travel along the lake shore of the Gouthwaite Reservoir (plate v). This is largely acid hill country and the eastern hill tops are clothed with Heather *(Calluna vulgaris)*. These lower slopes of Nidderdale are quite well wooded, though mainly forestry plantations. The remaining hillsides are a patchwortk of meadow and crop fields separated by the familiar intricate pattern of the dry-stone walls. The Yorkshire Water Authority's Gouthwaite Reservoir is a nature reserve of predominantly ornithological interest. The valley may not have the botanical riches of the limestone to the west, but the hillsides overlooking the reservoir, or verges close to the road, have a good variety of herbs:-

Angelica	*Angelica sylvestris*
Meadow Vetchling	*Lathyrus pratensis*
Meadowsweet	*Filipendula ulmaria*
Bush Vetch	*Vicia sepium*
Greater Burnet Saxifrage	*Pimpinella major*
Wood Cranesbill	*Geranium sylvaticum*
Lady's Mantle	*Alchemilla sp.*

Greater Burnet Saxifrage *(Pimpinella major)* is often a difficult plant to identify. It is a white, almost hairless late flowering member of the *Umbelliferae* which has attractive dark green foliage. As with its smaller relative, Burnet Saxifrage *(Pimpinella saxifraga)*, the pin-

PLATE v
Gouthwaite Reservoir.

nate leaves become finer as you travel up the stem. The larger, lower leaves have broad leaflets, coarse foliage when compared with the delicate, acute compound leaves of the middle stem. The importance of each leaf type often varies dramatically from plant to plant, area to area. In effect the plant has several disguises and most textbook illustrations give only one aspect of this multi-faceted flower. Wood Cranesbill *(Geranium sylvaticum)* is a showy, pink geranium that flowers early in the spring, and in late summer these shades are provided by the conspicuous spikes of Betony *(Betonica officinalis* plate 6a*)*. The flowers of the cranesbill are a similar size to its more purple relative, Meadow Cranesbill *(Geranium pratense)*. Many people can separate the two on flower colour alone, they can retain the pink-purple distinction in their mind and recognise each in the absence of the other. It is also true that Wood Cranesbill has white-centred bold flowers that look up to the summer sky, compared with the more reticent Meadow Cranesbill whose flowers glance sideways at their neighbours in the grass. The two flowers and foliage are illustrated in Figure 4. In the past I have had to rely on

FIGURE 4

A Meadow Cranesbill
(Geranium pratense)

B Wood Cranesbill
(Geranium sylvaticum)

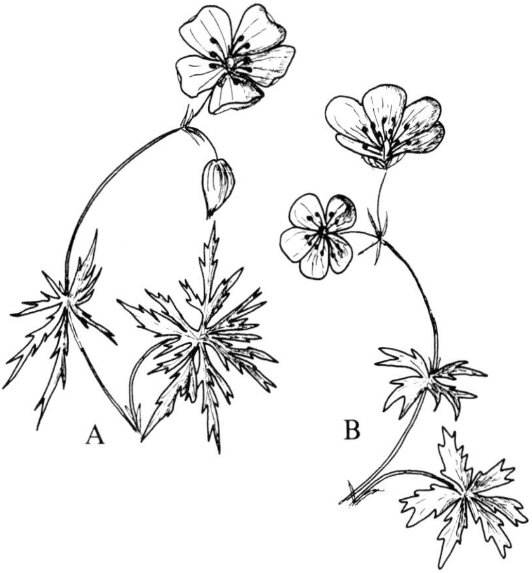

foliage shape to make a certain identification; there are reliable and clear differences in leaf lobe shape.

One soon climbs above the tree-lined reservoir to follow the natural course of the river Nidd. The river is also lined by trees and where Alder *(Alnus glutinosa)* and Willow *(Salix sp)* separate the river bank is carpeted in Butterbur *(Petasites hybridus)* and Sweet Cicely *(Myrrhis odorata)*. The Yorkshire Water Authority has another reservoir area high in the hills. The road to the Scar House Reservoir is open to the public, and passes some very interesting grasslands (plate vii). An increasing calcareous influence on some banks is evidenced by the occurrence of several calcicole (lime loving) plants.

Hairy St. John's Wort	*Hypericum hirsutum*
Rough Hawkbit	*Leontodon hispidus*
Quaking Grass	*Briza media*
Wood False Brome	*Brachypodium sylvaticum*
Fairy Flax	*Linum catharticum*
Ox Eye Daisy	*Chrysanthemum leucanthemum*
Pignut	*Conopodium majus*

These plants grow with other grassland herbs which are less indicative of lime.

Agrimony	*Agrimonia eupatoria*
Harebell	*Campanula rotundifolia*
Common Forget-me-not	*Myosotis arvense*
Bird's Foot Trefoil	*Lotus corniculatus*
Wild Strawberry	*Fragaria vesca*
Hard Heads	*Centaurea nigra*
Mouse Ear Chickweed	*Cerastium fontanum*
Common Spotted Orchid	*Dactylorhiza fuchsii*
Water Avens	*Geum rivale*
Tormentil	*Potentilla erecta*
Common St. John's Wort	*Hypericum perforatum*

The complex nature of these communities of flowers is confirmed by the occurrence close by of lime-hating (calcifuge) plants.

Beautiful St. John's Wort	*Hypericum pulchrum*
Bilberry	*Vaccinium myrtillus*
Heather	*Calluna vulgaris*
Devil's Bit Scabious	*Succisa pratensis*

In disturbed soils near an old railway line Quaking Grass *(Briza media)* and Heather grow together, oblivious that they are breaking the basic rules of habitat preference as expressed in plant ecological textbooks. It is likely that the plants are actually rooted at different depths, the Heather in acid soils, and the Quaking Grass in more neutral soil. We have not completed our list of interesting flowers and grasses along this particular stretch of Nidderdale. In these grassy banks we can also find flowers which are usually found in the shelter of woodland. Presumably these plants are persisting after woodland clearance in the immediate area.

Broad Buckler Fern	*Dryopteris dilitata*
Red Campion	*Silene dioica*
Dog's Mercury	*Mercurialis perennis*
Wood Sorrel	*Oxalis acetosella*
Wood Avens	*Geum urbanum*

This is a peaceful and attractive landscape, illustrated in plate vii. The steep climb out of Nidderdale brings one to the eastern slopes of the Pennines. The distant view is across the Vale of Mowbray to the Cleveland Hills. The immediate vistas are Heather clad grouse moor, very reminiscent of the North Yorkshire Moors which continue east from these Cleveland Hills. The Atlantic rain storms usually exhaust themselves on the western hills and by the time these winds reach this leeward side of the Pennines they carry much less moisture. Heather is favoured by this drier environment and in August the moors are vivid, purple carpets of colour, broken by bright green patches of Bilberry *(Vaccinium myrtillus)*. The river Burn rises close to the Scar House Reservoir and the river Nidd. The Nidd flows south to Pateley Bridge, but the Burn takes its course east down the foot-hills of the Pennines flowing through the short valley called Colsterdale. These are quiet environs, little frequented by holiday-makers who prefer the wider, busier valley of Wensleydale a little to the north. Often the lonely farmsteads lie close to the narrow lane, which is lined with magnificent old Ash *(Fraxinus excelsior)* trees. The frequency of Feverfew *(Chrysanthemum parthenium)* is a noticeable feature of farm-yard and village green. This is a common flower of dry waste places which has often been cultivated for its medicinal uses as well as for the attractive white and yellow flowers. Numerous streams feed into the river Burn and whether you look in wet ditch or by flowing torrent you may find several wet site species.

Fool's Water Cress	*Apium nodiflorum*
Brooklime	*Veronica beccabunga*
Golden Saxifrage	*Chrysosplenium oppositifolium*
Marsh Stitchwort	*Stellaria palustris*
Short Fuited Willow Herb	*Epilobium obscurum*
Marsh Bird's Foot Trefoil	*Lotus uliginosus*
Marsh Thistle	*Cirsium palustre*

Marsh Bird's Foot Trefoil *(Lotus uliginosus)* can be distinguished from the drier site relative, Bird's Foot Trefoil *(L. corniculatus)*, by the brown, reflexed calyx teeth which are evident around the buds of the wet-site species.

From Colsterdale the river Burn flows down towards Masham where it joins the Ure. It passes through that botanically rich rock, the magnesian limestone. The flowers here I relate to the journey of the great river Ure and describe them in the chapter on Wensleydale.

FACTS AND FICTION

Betony *(Betonica officinalis).*
The specific epithet 'officinalis' denotes important medicinal plants that were sold in herbal shops in the Middle Ages. In this period Betony was often cultivated in monastery gardens and used in treatment of many different illnesses from jaundice to dog bites. A herbal tea was made from the dried leaves, which were also smoked as tobacco. With all these helpful attributes it is not surprising that the plant was thought a lucky talisman and fragments were worn round the neck to ward off evil spirits. This is not a popular herb of present day herbalists.

Feverfew *(Chrysanthemum parthenium).*
The common name is thought to be a mispronunciation of "febrifuge", a remedy for fever. Indeed this is an ancient medicinal plant which is still used by herbalists today. It is credited with powers to ease colic, aid digestion and as a general tonic, and recently has been recommended for migraine sufferers, either to make a tea with the leaves or simply to chew on the raw bitter leaf. Feverfew is often found around gardens and is my favourite, uninvited visitor to herbaceous borders.

Common St. John's Wort *(Hypericum perforatum).*
The leaves are covered with pellucid dots which appear like tiny holes. From the Doctrine of Signatures this was suggested as a cure for wounds and during the Crusades the Knights of St. John of Jerusalem used the plant for this purpose. Alternatively the red sap of the plant was thought to represent the blood of St. John. Whatever the origins of the name, during the Middle Ages the plant was held to have great magical and protective properties. Juice from the plant is antiseptic and is used to prepare soothing ointments for sores.

a)

b)

PLATE 1

a) Monkey-Flower *(Mimulus guttatus)* Perennial herb up to 30 cm; naturalised and common by rivers; flowers 2.5-3.5cm. from June.

b) Foxglove *(Digitalis purpurea)* Biennial herb up to 150cm; leaves 15-30cm; common on acid soils; flowers 4-5cm. from June.

c) Flag *(Iris pseudacorus)* Bulbous herb up to 100cm; frequent in wet places; flowers 8-10cm. from May.

c)

a)

b)

c)

PLATE 2.

a) Mountain Everlasting *(Antennaria dioica)* Perennial creeping herb; Uncommon on dry rocky sites; flower head shown is female, male is white; from late May.

b) Caraway *(Carum carvi)* Hairless biennial 25-60cm; narrow leaf segments of compound leaves; rare, naturalised escape; flowers 2-3mm. from June.

c) Herb Paris *(Paris quadrifolia)* Perennial herb 15-40cm; uncommon in calcareous woods; flower 2.5-3.5cm; early May to July.

a)

PLATE 3

a) Thrift *(Armeria maritima)* Perennial herb forming cushions of linear flowers; uncommon by streams in upland pastures; flowers (8mm.) in dense heads from May.

b) Horseshoe Vetch *(Hippocrepis comosa)* Perennial herb; 10-40cm; pinnate leaves; occasional on dry limestone; flowers 1cm. several in round head in May.

c) Spring Gentian *(Gentiana verna)* Perennial herb up to 6cm; leaves in rosette; many populations in Upper Teesdale; flowers 2.5cm. in late May.

b)

c)

a)

b)

c)

PLATE 4

a) Tea Leaved Willow *(Salix phylicifolia)* Shrub up to 4m; with shining leaves of 2-8cm; local on wet rocks by streams; flowers April-May.

b) Mountain Avens *(Dryas octapetala)* Creeping evergreen undershrub with crinkled leaves; rare on high fells; flowers 2.5-4cm. in June.

c) Bird's Eye Primrose *(Primula farinosa)* Perennial herb up to 15cm; leaves in basal rosettes frequent in calcareous wetland; flowers May.

a)

b)

c)

PLATE 5

a) Green Winged Orchid *(Orchis morio)* Flower stems 10-30cm; uncommon in permanent pasture; spike of flowers 3-8cm. in May.

b) Mountain Pansy *(Viola lutea)* Perennial herb 7-15cm; also purple or yellow-purple; common on leached limestone grassland; flowers 2.5-3cm. in May.

c) Early Marsh Orchid *(Orchis incarnata)* Flower stem 15-50cm; perennial orchid of calcareous wetland; flowers mid June to mid July.

PLATE 6

a) Betony *(Betonica officinalis)* Perennial herb 15-45cm; frequent in limestone pastures; flowers 1.5cm. in dense heads from late June.
b) Bird Cherry *(Prunus padus)* Deciduous tree 3-15m; common in woods and by streams; racemes of 10-40 flowers in May.
c) Wild Thyme *(Thymus drucei)* Creeping perennial with small opposite aromatic leaves; common in grassland; flowers from June.

a)

b)

c)

a)

b)

c)

PLATE 7

a) Lesser Club Moss *(Selaginella selaginoides)* A fern with stems usually 3-8cm; minute spiral leaves; frequent in short limestone grassland.

b) Bloody Cranesbill *(Geranium sanguineum)* Perennial herb 10-40cm; flowers borne singly; frequent among limestone rocks; flowers 3cm. from June.

c) Yellow Mountain Saxifrage *(Saxifraga aizoides)* Perennial herb 5-20cm; succulent leaves; red stem; occasional on wet stony ground; flower 1.5cm. in July.

a)

b)

PLATE 8

a) Purple Saxifrage *(Saxifraga oppositifolia)* Perennial herb; long trailing stems with tiny leaves; rare at high altitudes on limestone; flower 2cm. late April.

b) Broad Buckler Fern *(Dryopteris dilitata)* A robust fern with fronds up to 150cm; dies back in autumn; common in woodland, pavements and shady places.

c) Common Rockrose *(Helinathemum chamaecitus)* Perennial trailing shrub 5-30cm; small glossy leaves; common on limestone; flowers 2cm. from June.

c)

a)

b)

c)

PLATE 9

a) Baneberry *(Actaea spicata)* Perennial herb; 30-65cm; black poisonous berries; local in woods and pavement; flowers in May.

b) Marjoram *(Origanum vulgare)* Sweet-smelling perennial 30-80cm; common on limestone; flowers 6-8mm. from July.

c) Sundew *(Drosera rotundifolia)* Perennial herb 6-25cm. leaves with glandular hairs that trap flies; frequent in bogs; flowers, tiny, white in July.

a)

b)

c)

PLATE 10

a) Felwort *(Gentianella amarella)* Biennial herb around 10cm; frequent in dry pastures; flowers 1cm, 4 or 5 petals from late July.

b) Yellow Rattle *(Rhinanthus minor)* and Goat's Beard *(Tragopogon minor)*. Yellow herbs of pasture and hay meadow; common throughout the Dales; flowers from June.

c) Alpine Bartsia *(Bartsia alpina)* Perennial herb 10-20cm. very hairy; rare in uplands; flowers up to 2cm. June-July.

a)

PLATE 11

a) Bird's Nest Orchid *(Neottia nidus-avis)* Saprophytic with no green leaves; stem 20-45cm; rare in Beech woods flowering in June.

b) Storksbill *(Erodium cicutarium)* Annual up to 60cm; long pointed fruits; pinnate leaves; common on dry soils; flowers 1cm. from May.

c) False Oxslip *(Primula veris x vulgaris)* A variable hybrid between primrose and cowslip; quite common where they meet; flowers in May.

b)

c)

a)

b)

c)

PLATE 12

a) Burnt Tip Orchid *(Orchis ustulata)* Flower stem 8-20cm. rare in permanent pasture; flower spike 2-5cm. in May-June.

b) Squinancywort *(Asperula cynanchica)* Perennial prostrate herb; local in grassland on magnesian limestone; flowers 6mm. in July-August.

c) Early Purple Orchid *(Orchis mascula)* Flower stem 15-50cm; frequent in woodlands, less common in meadows; spike of flowers 4-15cm. in April-May.

RIBBLESDALE AND THE THREE PEAKS

Yorkshire's only true claim to the alpine environment lies with the windswept summits of the Three Peaks: Ingleborough, Penyghent and Whernside. At altitudes of 723, 694, and 736 metres, these hills extend well above tree line into the alpine zone. The mountain flowers of these peaks are found on the high altitude limestone cliffs and not necessarily on the summits themselves which are capped with the acid, unrewarding rock of millstone grit. Nature Conservancy records list several mountain flowers for the slopes of the Three Peaks.

PLATE vi
Melancholy Thistle
(Cirsium heterophyllum).

Alpine Cinquefoil	*Potentilla crantzii*
Alpine Saw-wort	*Saussaurea alpina*
English Sandwort	*Arenaria norvegica ssp. anglica*
Alpine Bistort	*Polygonum viviparum*
Alpine Poa	*Poa alpina*

These alpines are rather difficult to find, but for the enthusiast who climbs Penyghent or Ingleborough at Easter the flowering of the Purple Saxifrage *(Saxifraga oppositifolia* plate 8a*)* will reward his efforts. At this time while most of the valley rests under a winter garb, and snow still clings to the rocky slopes, the coronet of limestone cliffs beneath the crown of millstone grit is decked with the beautiful flowers of Purple Saxifrage. The flowers form vivid clusters against the white rocks and can truly be considered as one of Britain's most attractive native alpines. Plate 8a was photographed on our last visit to Penyghent. After the late, cold spring of 1986 we were fortunate to choose a warm April day with deep blue skies and clear distant views. The sparkling vernal sunshine exaggerated the brilliance of the purple flowers against their rocky habitat, altogether a perfect day.

A visitor to Penyghent in early spring, who climbs to see the Purple Saxifrage will not see many other plants in flower, but he can find:

Spring Whitlow Grass	*Erophila verna*
Blue Mountain Grass	*Sesleria caerulea*
Town Hall Clock	*Adoxa moschatelina*
Hare's Tail Cotton Grass	*Eriophorum vaginatum*

The chaff-coloured fruiting heads of Sesleria wave over the Pennine turf throughout the long summer, but the vivid blue of the grass head in April flower may come as a surprise to many. The relationship of Hare's Tail Cotton Grass with the true sedges is very clear when one examines the springtime flowering head, as it shows anthers to the April wind. The cottony heads of summer that give the plant its common name are of very different appearance.

The numerous pot-holes and sink-holes on the lower slopes of these hills are rich fern gardens where fronds thrive in the cool damp hollows. The northern route up Penyghent from Horton-in-Ribblesdale follows the Pennine Way. Just off the path is Hunt Pot, where

PLATE vii
Upper Reaches of Nidderdale.

water cascades into a deep cavern and the wet rocks support many interesting ferns and higher plants. Golden Saxifrage *(Chrysosplenium oppositifolium)* and Yellow Mountain Saxifrage *(Saxifraga aizoides* plate 7c*)* glisten under the sprays of water from the rock sides. Mossy Saxifrage *(Saxifraga hypnoides* plate iv*)* flourishes on the drier rocks and from here it follows the Purple Saxifrage to the highest precipice. As we have seen in previous chapters Mossy Saxifrage occurs in many areas in the Dales, and often in contrasting habitats: waterfall rocks in Swaledale, the edge of lead spoil near Kettlewell, loose boulder slopes on Penyghent. The slopes of Simon Fell lead west out of Ribblesdale and over to Ingleborough. On this hillside can be found yet another habitat for this successful saxifrage, namely grassy limestone pavement. This pavement is the National Nature Reserve of Colt Park Wood and is the habitat for many other interesting plants. The reserve encloses a thin strip of vegetated limestone pavement which contours round the fell at a little over 305m. On a dais of limestone pavement the reserve was naturally little grazed, and is now fenced to preclude sheep. The absence of sheep allows a lush herb layer under scattered trees of:-

Ash	*Fraxinus excelsior*
Birch	*Betula pendula*
Wych Elm	*Ulmus glabra*
Hazel	*Corylus avellana*
Bird Cherry	*Prunus padus*
Rowan	*Sorbus aucuparia*

On my two most recent visits sheep were entering the southern parts of the reserve. The athletic feats of sheep in search of grazing are a constant problem in the conservation of wild flowers of upland rocky habitats. Colt Park is a closed reserve which means permission must be sought from the Nature Conservancy before visiting. This reserve represents a very unique aspect of pavement woodland. Many slabs are still covered with Blue Mountain Grass turf and herbaceous carpets cover hidden grikes and hollows. The visitor should be very cautious and tread warily. Representative plants that I have recorded include:-

Small Scabious	*Scabiosa columbaria*
Bloody Cranesbill	*Geranium sanguineum*
Wood Cranesbill	*G. sylvaticum*
Wild Garlic	*Allium ursinum*
Bluebell	*Hyacinthoides non-scripta*
Melancholy Thistle	*Cirsium heterophyllum*
Mossy Saxifrage	*Saxifraga hypnoides*
Rockrose	*Helianthemum chamaecistus*
Salad Burnet	*Poterium sanguisorba*
Meadow Sweet	*Filipendula ulmaria*
Lesser Meadow Rue	*Thalictrum minus*
Dog's Mercury	*Mercurialis perennis*
Wood Sanicle	*Sanicula europaea*
Wood Anemone	*Anemone nemorosa*
Globe Flower	*Trollius europaeus*
Baneberry	*Actaea spicata*
Water Avens	*Geum rivale*
Angelica	*Angelica sylvestris*
Greater Bellflower	*Campanula latifolia*

PLATE viii
Limestone Pavement near Malham.

Common Valerian	*Valeriana officinalis*
Wall Lettuce	*Mycelis muralis*
Lily of the Valley	*Convallaria majalis*
Greater Burnet	*Sanguisorba officinalis*
Lady's Bedstraw	*Galium verum*

This list of flowers does not cover the full range of species that can be found in this very rich area. The fern flora of this pavement is extensive, and this is equally true of the Yorkshire Wildlife Trust Reserve at South House Pavement which lies nearer to Horton-in-Ribblesdale on this same side of the valley. Look for the elusive Holly Fern *(Polystichum lonchitis)* nestling deep within a shady grike, or on more sunlit pavements the primitive Moonwort *(Botrychium lunaria* Figure 2*)*.

On the opposite side of Ribblesdale, Ling Gill National Nature Reserve is centred on a steep-sided and wooded ravine. This topography has given natural protection from grazing and the vegetation is very lush. The terrain is of course equally difficult for the visitor.

In summary the most interesting areas around Ribblesdale are those which are not grazed by sheep, namely high limestone cliffs, protected pavement or deep pot-holes and the churchyard at Horton itself is worth a look (plate iii)! These habitats provide a dramatic environmental contrast, high illumination on the cliff, perpetual shade in the pot-hole, windswept summits versus tranquil corridors in the grike. The variety of habitat leads to a diverse flora. Contrasting climates give a long flowering season across the valley. The precocious alpines flower from April, yet in the cool pot-hole the season is delayed. When we climbed Ingleborough on a shimmering hot July day we saw Bugle *(Ajuga reptans)* in flower deep in Fluted Hole, a woodland plant which we normally expect to flower in early June.

Botanising on the Three Peaks can never be a lonely expedition, but avoid the sponsored or competitive run-cycle-hike and the peaks themselves are well worth a visit. As your feet clatter across the wooden slats and steps which protect the lower slopes, it is incredible to reflect that the alpines high above you have looked across Ribblesdale for nearly 10,000 years. They have seen the valley clothed in woodland, the pastures emerge from its shadow and the diligent farmer build mile upon mile of dry stone wall to protect his inheritance, and finally with the advancing crowds of walkers have seen the hillsides scarred and eroded by thousands of feet.

FACTS AND FICTION

Golden Saxifrage *(Chrysosplenium oppositifolium).*
The name saxifrage means stone-breaker, and refers to the frequently rocky habitat of this group. Golden Saxifrage is perhaps more characteristic of stream-side sites or crevices flushed with water. This genus is very different from most other saxifrages, by having flower parts in fours instead of five and in the absence of showy petals. The foliage is edible raw and is still apparently eaten in salads in parts of France!

Greater Burnet *(Sanguisorba officinalis).*
This plant was once a familiar sight in hay meadows, but with the destruction of its habitat it is becoming more scarce. The Latin name "sanguisorba" means blood ball and refers to the colour and shape of the flower cluster. This is an old medicinal plant, its roots containing tannins and saponin. The flower heads were used in recipes for country wine.

Lady's Bedstraw *(Galium verum).*
A source of coumarin which is used medicinally in drugs to treat heart disease. The chemical smells of new-mown hay and is a sedative. The common name comes from the legend that Mary was lying on a bed of this plant when she gave birth to Jesus, thus benefitting from its narcotic properties. Popular with herbalists as an external healer of ulcers and dermatitis and internally for migraine. The plant also contains rennet. This is the enzyme used to curdle milk, and Lady's Bedstraw was used in cheese-making.

MALHAM TO LITTONDALE

The seven mile walk from Malham village up Gordale Scar to the tarn and back to the village via Malham Cove must be one of the most scenic walks in the Yorkshire Dales. In dry weather the climb up Gordale is not difficult, but at all times this is a most spectacular chasm between limestone walls which tower up to 90 metres on either side. The path follows the steep stream bed upwards through what was once a narrow cave. For those less agile a narrow road network follows a similar route from Malham to the tarn. The moor around the tarn has a mosaic of varying soil types reflecting their different glacial histories. There are soils derived from weathering limestone and these are shallow and calcareous. In many areas boulder clay was dropped over the limestone by retreating glaciers, and where drainage was impeded peat has accumulated over water-logged soils. The plant species in this small area cover the whole ecological range of upland types from those characteristic of dry or wet alkaline soils to those found on the wet acid conditions of Malham Tarn Bog. The fast-flowing calcareous streams cascading from the moor have interesting waterside vegetation. Bird's Eye Primrose *(Primula farinosa* plate 4c*)* is frequent on disturbed stream-side banks.
Other flowers to look for include:-

Knotted Pearlwort	*Sagina nodosa*
Lesser Clubmoss	*Selaginella selaginoides*
Water Avens	*Geum rivale*
Marsh Ragwort	*Senecio aquaticus*
Grass of Parnassus	*Parnassia palustris*
Alpine Scurvy Grass	*Cochlearia alpina*

For those who are only familiar with the tiny petal-less pearlwort of garden path and lawn (*Sagina apetala* and *procumbens*) the showy white flowers of Knotted Pearlwort *(Sagina nodosa)* will be quite

PLATE ix
Yew Cogar Scar, Littondale.

FIGURE 5

A Felwort
(Gentianella amarella)

B Field Gentian
(Gentianella campestris)

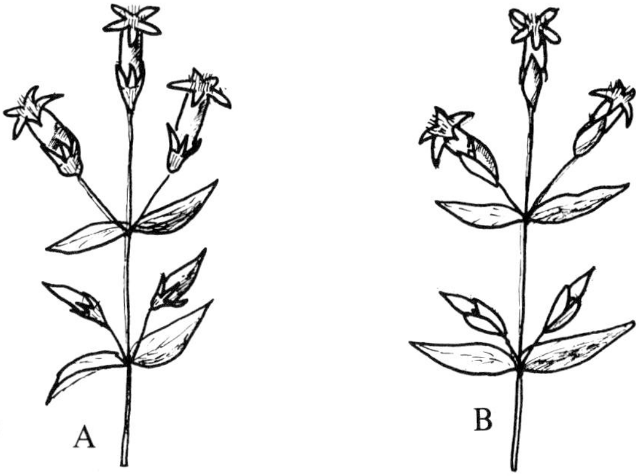

surprising. The common name comes from the clustered leaves which are spaced along the stem like knots. Knotted Pearlwort flowers late in the summer, and at this same time look out for the dull, purple flowers of Felwort *(Gentianella amarella* plate 10a*)*. This little gentian prefers disturbed sites with little competition from vigorous grasses. It can be distinguished from its relative Field Gentian *(Gentianella campestris)* by examining the shape of the calyx. Equal teeth surround the flower of the Felwort, whereas in Field Gentian two of the teeth are greatly enlarged and overlap the rest (Figure 5). The latter is a more unusual plant to find preferring acid sites, but both can be found in many areas in the Dales.

Where calcareous flushes fan out across the moor a more stable wetland community has developed, rich in sedges and herbaceous wetland species and varying in acidity.

Water Cress	*Nasturtium officinale*
Brooklime	*Veronica beccabunga*
Marsh Marigold	*Caltha palustris*
Marsh Bedstraw	*Galium palustre*
Lesser Spearwort	*Ranunculus flammula*
Red Rattle	*Pedicularis palustris*
Bog Bean	*Menyanthes trifoliata*
Common Spotted Orchid	*Dactylorhiza fuchsii*
Northern Marsh Orchid	*D. purpurella*
Marsh Cinquefoil	*Potentilla palustris*
Common Sundew	*Droser rotundifolia*

Red Rattle *(Pedicularis palustris)* is also given the name Marsh Lousewort, indicating a similarity with its smaller relative Common Lousewort *(Pedicularis sylvatica)*. Common Lousewort can be found close by in the rough grassland over boulder clay soils, dominated by Mat Grass *(Nardus stricta)* and Heath Rush *(Juncus squarrosus)*. Although Red Rattle is usually taller and more conspicuous, separation of the two can be certain when examining the calyx tube behind the flower, hairless in Lousewort and very hairy in Red Rattle.

Malham Tarn itself is one of only three natural lakes in Yorkshire, a surprising scarcity of natural open water in such a large county. Even before Local Government re-organisation the old boundaries of Yorkshire included only four lakes: Malham Tarn, Semerwater, Gormire Lake under Sutton Bank near Thirsk and Hornsea Mere on the Yorkshire coast. Hornsea is now included in Humberside. All these lakes are quite small; the Tarn covers 61 hectares with a maximum depth of only 4.2m, lies at an altitude of about 365m and is the highest marl lake (calcareous mud) in Britain. In the late 18th century Lord Ribblesdale dammed the lake to raise the level and he planted many trees around the water's edge. This whole area was used by the great monastic sheep herds which grazed over the treeless landscape and whose influence lasted for four centuries. The land here was divided between the two great monasteries of Fountains Abbey and Bolton Abbey. The northern bank of the Tarn is National Trust Property, leased to the Field Studies Council, who offer a wide range of courses from Tarn House. The house was built in the 19th century by Walter Morrison. Many distinguished visitors came to Tarn House and perhaps the most remembered is Charles Kingsley whose idea for the 'Water Babies' is said to have evolved with the crystal clear streams and savage precipice of Malham Cove.

The western edge of the Tarn comes within National Trust Boundaries and has a complex, raised acid bog partially surrounded by fen vegetation. The presence of Bog Rosemary *(Andromeda polifolia)* is evidence that the bog surface has been little disturbed by man, since this is one of the first species to disappear in bogs where man has grazed, drained or burned the vegetation. The whole is a very ancient site, graded as of supreme importance by the Nature Conservancy Council. There is no public access to the western end of the Tarn.

Dropping below the Tarn on our route back to Malham village we are now walking through dry limestone turf and rocky outcrops.

The water from the Tarn disappears from view at Water Sinks (849655) and rises at Airhead Springs south of Malham. Water flowing into the stream below the cove comes not from the Tarn but from Smelt Mill Sinks (882659). In springtime the grassland will be dotted with Mountain Pansy *(Viola lutea* plate 5b*)*, Eyebright *(Euphrasia officinalis)* and Wild Thyme *(Thymus drucei* plate 6c*)*. Where grazing pressure is reduced look for the beautiful white flowers of Meadow Saxifrage *(Saxifraga granulata)*. Here also are several areas of limestone pavement (plate viii), where woodland flowers find a shady refuge, and ferns grow layer-upon-layer down into the deepest grike. Baneberry *(Actaea spicata* plate 9a*)* grows in these pavements, its white flowers appearing in May. This very poisonous plant is of limited distribution, being restricted to Yorkshire, Lancashire and Westmorland. Above the pavements the rocky terrain has many ungrazed cliffs which support a characteristic calcareous flora:-

Marjoram	*Origanum vulgare*
Orpine	*Sedum telephinum*
Burnet Saxifrage	*Pimpinella saxifraga*
Small Scabious	*Scabiosa columbaria*
Wood Sage	*Teucrium scorodonia*
Rockrose	*Helianthemum chamaecistus*
Lesser Meadow Rue	*Thalictrum minus*
Rock Whitebeam	*Sorbus rupicola*
Wall Lettuce	*Mycelis muralis*
Golden Rod	*Solidago virgaurea*
Harebell	*Campanula rotundifolia*
Hairy Rock Cress	*Arabis hirsuta*
Wild Basil	*Clinopodium vulgare*
Three Fingered Saxifrage	*Saxifraga tridactylites*

Wild Jacob's Ladder *(Polemonium caeruleum)* is still found in the area. Familiar to many as a garden plant the native species has become quite rare and difficult to find. Limestone crags are the best habitat for another northern plant, the Dark Red Helleborine *(Epipactis atrorubens)*. Sensitive to grazing the finest specimens can be seen in sheltered hollows on precipitous cliffs, safe from herbivore or collector. This orchid flowers in mid-summer and is an elusive member of the limestone flora. I have often thought that it becomes more common on the remote Scottish Cambrian limestones. At

PLATE x
Malham Cove.

Malham Cove the Great Scar Limestone is exposed across the mid-craven fault. The limestone pavement at the top of the cove still has an interesting flora despite visitor pressure. Deep in the shady grikes the wild flowers are protected from trampling feet, subject only to the indignity of falling beer cans or crisp packets. The naturalist needs no excuse to climb the cove, the view is breath-taking, the adjacent cliffs fascinating, the whole is a unique experience that should not be missed.

The route over the 73 metre high cove forms part of the Pennine Way, and the slopes below the cove are too well used to support any but the commonest grassland flowers.

From Malham narrow roads to the north connect Ribblesdale with Littondale. At the junction of these routes lies one of the smallest reserves of the Yorkshire Wildlife Trust, Globe Flower Wood: a small corner protected by high stone walls, an oasis of luxuriant herbs that is surrounded by hillsides cropped short by sheep. A small, shady fragment dominated by glorious Globeflower *(Trollius europaeus* front cover*)*, but splashed pink with Wood Cranesbill *(Geranium sylvaticum)*, Water Avens *(Geum rivale)* and Melancholy Thistle *(Cirsium heterophyllum* plate vi*)*, and white with Sweet Cicely *(Myrrhis odorata)*. You can find these same species massed in hay meadows which lie north of this reserve, over the fells high in Littondale, almost at the source of the river Skirfare. Such herb-rich meadows are scarce in this part of the Dales and typical flowers include:-

Butterbur	*Petasites hybridus*
Melancholy Thistle	*Cirsium heterophyllum*
Sweet Cicely	*Myrrhis odorata*
Water Avens	*Geum rivale*
Common Figwort	*Scrophularia nodosa*
Yellow Rattle	*Rhinanthus minor*
Greater Burnet	*Sanguisorba officinalis*
Milkmaid	*Cardamine pratensis*
Meadow Sweet	*Filipendula ulmaria*
Meadow Cranesbill	*Geranium pratense*
Hard Heads	*Centaurea nigra*
Common Bistort	*Polygonum bistorta*
Red Clover	*Trifolium pratense*
Primrose	*Primula vulgaris*
Meadow Buttercup	*Ranunculus acris*
Goatsbeard	*Tragopogon minor*

The riverside at Foxup is equally interesting with springtime flushes that are reminiscent of Teesdale. Marsh Valerian *(Valeriana dioica)*, Alpine Scurvy Grass *(Cochlearia alpina)*, Butterwort *(Pinguicula vulgaris)* and Bird's Eye Primrose bring May flowers to the water's edge. From the heights of Halton Gill, Littondale stretches out to the south-east, until it reaches the major valley of Wharfedale. From the picturesque village of Arncliffe one can climb on either side of the valley to reach limestone scars and exceptional views of this dramatic scenery. The climb above Yew Cogar is particularly exciting. The path lies above high crags dotted with Yew *(Taxus baccata)* and Juniper *(Juniperus communis)* and steep enough to have formed an ideal refuge for the late glacial flora (plate ix). Far beneath

PLATE xi
Langstrothdale.

is the Cowside Beck whose waters join the main river Skirfare at Arncliffe.

These steep-sided valleys are some of the most remote areas in the Dales, where the naturalist can still hope to find the unexpected, overlooked rarity, among the rocks and boulders plucked and weathered by the Pleistocene ice.

FACTS AND FICTION

Sweet Cicely *(Myrrhis odorata).*
Every part of this pretty white umbel has been used by man. The foliage and seeds smell strongly of aniseed and the latter have been ground and incorporated with wax to make scented furniture polish. The boiled leaves are a green vegetable and the roots can also be cooked in this same way.

Common Figwort *(Scrophularia nodosa).*
The root has lumps which resemble the hard, eruptive swelling of the disease scrophula. From the Doctrine of Signatures the plant was therefore used to cure this disease. Figwort was also used to cure ulcers and other skin complaints. The purple flowers are attractive to many insects, including the larvae of the figwort weevil which eats the leaves and seed capsules of the plant.

Butterbur *(Petasites hybridus).*
Although the male Butterbur is common throughout England, the female plants are much more restricted, but do occur in Yorkshire. In olden times the leaves were used to wrap butter, and these leaves are very large (up to 1 metre across). The powdered root has been used to remove spots from the skin.

ARTIFICIAL HABITATS

In the preceding chapters I have described several artificial habitats associated with the various Dales eg. Preston Quarry in Wensleydale and lead spoil heaps in Wharfedale. Artificial habitats to the east of the Pennines have particular botanical interest, where the undulating landscape lies over magnesian limestone. This rock has weathered over the centuries to give light fertile soils, in a mild environment which is protected from the strong westerly winds by the high hills above the Dales. This area is extensively cultivated and tracts of wilderness are few. Thus it follows that in magnesian limestone country, artificial habitats become of great importance as refuges for wild flowers. The ruin of Jervaux is fashioned in this rock and this largely explains the floristic wealth. Another great abbey to the south has even more to offer than Jervaux. The sheep flocks from Fountains Abbey had a profound influence on the floristic character of thousands of acres of Pennine grassland during several centuries. Today Fountains Abbey is important for another reason: the abbey and grounds have an exceptional variety of wild flowers from a common speedwell on the ruined walls to a rare orchid in the surrounding woodland.

The rough contours of the ruined stones often form an irregular staircase which rises to the summit of the highest wall. Each tread harbours pockets of soil composed of wind-blown particles and weathering stone. Where there is soil there are flowers, small, tall, common, rare; of delicate pink or brilliant blue, a monastery garden of every colour. Several of the flowers that are naturalised on the walls are not part of our native flora, but ancient garden blooms that were originally cultivated by the ancient clerics. The most famous of these is the Common Pink *(Dianthus plumarius)*, but the walls are also decorated with a profusion of common Wallflowers *(Cheiranthus cheiri)*. Individually the flowers of the walls are short lived, but for three hundred years successive generations of plants have lived within this quiet sanctuary. Beyond the confines of this great ruin the many ages of restless man have extended the boundaries of our knowledge and understanding, achieving the advanced technology that we have today. But within the broken stone and high on fragmented towers the wild flowers of Fountains Abbey have not felt the passing of the years, but flourish now in gay abundance as they once flowered for the devoted monks.

The abbey grounds enclose a variety of habitats, the ruined walls themselves, calcareous grassland, aquatic and waterside vegetation and woodland. A full list of plant species is far too long to be included here; we must be content with a look at the most characteristic species.

The walls themselves

Time and weathering have created many pockets among the stones where wild flowers can flourish. It is clear that formerly the Ministry of Works and more recently the National Trust have been sympathetic to the wild flora of the grounds and have not encouraged over zealous gardening.

Flowers you will encounter:-

Ivy Leaved Toadflax	*Cymbalaria muralis*
Herb Robert	*Geranium robertianum*
Thale Cress	*Arabidopsis thaliana*
Spring Whitlow Grass	*Erophila verna*
Wall Lettuce	*Mycelis muralis*
Common Pink	*Dianthus plumarius*
Wallflower	*Cheiranthus cheiri*
Wall Speedwell	*Veronica arvensis*
Thyme Leaved Speedwell	*V. serpyllifolia*
Blue Fleabane	*Erigeron acer*
Hairy Rockcress	*Arabis hirsuta*
Hairy St. John's Wort	*Hypericum hirsutum*
Pellitory of the Wall	*Parietaria judaica*
Golden Rod	*Solidago virgaurea*
Fine Leaved Sandwort	*Minuartia hybrida*
Thyme Leaved Sandwort	*Arenaria serpyllifolia*
Marjoram	*Origanum vulgare*
Harebell	*Campanula rotundifolia*
Storksbill	*Erodium cicutarium*

FIGURE 6

A Wall Speedwell
(Veronica arvensis)

B Thyme-Leaved Speedwell
(Veronica serpyllifolia)

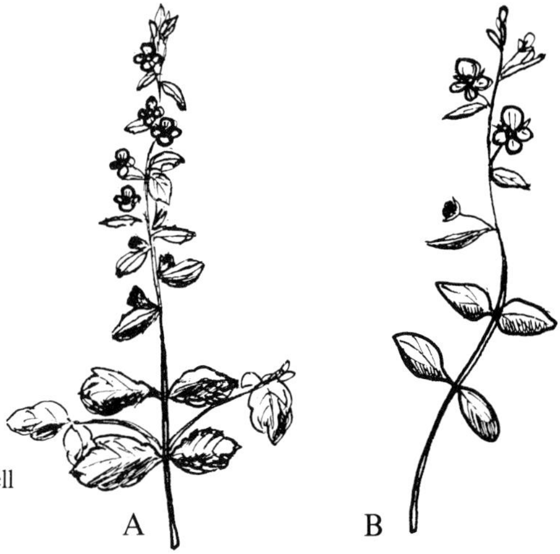

These flowers can survive on dry calcareous habitats, the stone walls of mid summer offering little water or protection from the sun. The two small speedwells (Wall and Thyme Leaved) are well adapted to grow in dry inhospitable habitats. They can be distinguished by differences in their leaf margin and the size of the flowers (Figure 6). Normally the flower of the Wall Speedwell is of the deepest blue, whereas Thyme Leaved Speedwell has a lilac-purple flower.

Nestling into shady corners and luxuriant in the darker hollows is a varied fern flora:-

Common Spleenwort	*Asplenium trichomanes*
Wall Rue	*A. ruta-muraria*
Common Polypody	*Polypodium vulgare*
Hart's Tongue Fern	*Phyllitis scolopendrium*
Brittle Bladder Fern	*Cystopteris fragilis*

The old water course approaches the edge of the buildings. Monkey Flower *(Mimulus guttatus* plate 1a*)* and Butterbur *(Petasites hybridus)* root in the shallow water, and gentle banks are pink and white with the tall vigorous growth of Great Hairy Willow Herb *(Epilobium hirsutum)*, Himalayan Balsam *(Impatiens glandulifera)* and Meadow Sweet *(Filipendula ulmaria)*. The aquatic and waterside flowers are very diverse, reflecting the antiquity of the canals and pools. Unfortunately the National Trust has had to undertake major works on these water-ways, with inevitable disturbance to marginal vegetation. We visited the ground during this work and were delighted to find all the flowers we had previously recorded. Reduced in number and clinging to overturned mud and retaining wall, but still providing the essential seed source for subsequent recolonisation once work has ceased:-

Himalayan Balsam	*Impatiens glandulifera*
Butterbur	*Petasites hybridus*
Meadow Sweet	*Filipendula ulmaria*
Water Figwort	*Scrophularia aquatica*
Great Hairy Willow Herb	*Epilobium hirsutum*
Common Valerian	*Valeriana officinalis*
Marsh Valerian	*V. dioica*
Water Avens	*Geum rivale*
Fen Bedstraw	*Galium uliginosum*
Marsh Bedstraw	*G. palustre*
Marsh Bird's Foot Trefoil	*Lotus uliginosus*
Bog Stitchwort	*Stellaria alsine*
Marsh Ragwort	*Senecio aquaticus*
Marsh Marigold	*Caltha palustris*
Marsh Stitchwort	*Stellaria palustris*
Bog Willow Herb	*Epilobium palustre*
Marsh Pennywort	*Hydrocotyle vulgaris*
Skullcap	*Scutellaria galericulata*
Square Stemmed St. John's Wort	*Hypericum tetrapterum*
Ragged Robin	*Lychnis flos-cuculi*
Wayside Cudweed	*Gnaphalium uliginosum*

Growing in the water:-

Monkey Flower	*Mimulus guttatus*
Water Plantain	*Alisma plantago-aquatica*
Water Forget-me-not	*Myosotis scorpioides*
Tufted Water Forget-me-not	*M. caespitosa*
Water Mint	*Mentha aquatica*
White Water Lily	*Nymphaea alba*
Spiked Water Milfoil	*Myriophyllum spicatum*

Amphibious Bistort	*Polygonum amphibium*
Brooklime	*Veronica beccabunga*
Water Cress	*Nasturtium officinale*
Water Crowfoot	*Ranunculus peltatus*

Marsh Bird's Foot Trefoil *(Lotus uliginosus)* can often be difficult to separate from Common Bird's Foot Trefoil *(L. corniculatus)*. Normally the wetland species is taller and more elongated, but habitat variation can camouflage this difference in growth form. Examine the buds of the flowers for a clear demarcation between the two. In bud the calyx teeth of Marsh Bird's Foot Trefoil are reflexed and stand away from the bud like brown bristles, whereas in the common species the teeth lie close to the bud.

The yellow-flowered Square Stemmed St. John's Wort *(Hypericum tetrapterum)* is usually found in damp sites. The flowers are less conspicuous than those of the three other St. John's Wort which are found at Fountains, although the floral shape of all members of this genera are strikingly similar. Hairy St. John's Wort is a plant of calcareous soils, Common St. John's Wort grows vigorously on many soils and Beautiful St. John's Wort is often found on more acid areas. Fountains Abbey has much to fascinate the observant botanist.

The woods that border the grounds offer several sites of mature Beech *(Fagus sylvatica)* woodland, ancient enough to be a habitat for the elusive Bird's Nest Orchid *(Neottis nidus-avis* plate 11a*)*. Many woodland flowers edge the paths which cross the grounds and it is clear that these are remnants of primary woodland.

Flowers of the woodland and woodland edge:-

Wild Garlic	*Allium ursinum*
Jack by-the-hedge	*Alliaria petiolata*
Wood Sanicle	*Sanicula europaea*
Dog's Mercury	*Mercurialis perennis*
Wood Avens	*Geum urbanum*
Mountain Currant	*Ribes alpinum*
Woodruff	*Asperula odorata*
Wood Sorrel	*Oxalis acetosella*
Wood Forget-me-not	*Myosotis sylvatica*
Three Nerved Sandwort	*Moerhingia trinervia*

Greater Bellflower	*Campanula latifolia*
Small Teasel	*Dipsacus pilosus*
Enchanter's Nightshade	*Circaea lutetiana*
Golden Saxifrage	*Chrysosplenium oppositifolia*
Deadly Nightshade	*Atropa bella-donna*
Wood Anemone	*Anemone nemorosa*
Yellow Pimpernel	*Lysimachia nemorum*
Wood Sage	*Teucrium scorodonia*
Primrose	*Primula vulgaris*

Areas of natural calcareous grassland are limited and scattered around the grounds. A high species diversity per given area is a general feature of such grasslands and consequently small fragments at Fountains add greatly to the overall species list.

Flowers of the grasslands:-

Greater Mullein	*Verbascum thapsus*
Zig Zag Clover	*Trifolium medium*
Hard Heads	*Centaurea nigra*
Hoary Plantain	*Plantago media*
Devil's Bit Scabious	*Succisa pratensis*
Small Scabious	*Scabiosa columbaria*
Ox Eye Daisy	*Chrysanthemum leucanthemum*
Common St. John's Wort	*Hypericum perforatum*
Common Lady's Mantle	*Alchemilla glabra agg.*
Wild Basil	*Clinopodium vulgare*
Common Calamint	*C. ascendens*
Eyebright	*Euphrasia officinalis*
Cowslip	*Primula veris*
Common Milkwort	*Polygala vulgaris*
Salad Burnet	*Poterium sanguisorba*
Wild Thyme	*Thymus drucei*
Betony	*Betonica officinalis*
Tormentil	*Potentilla erecta*
Rough Hawkbit	*Leontodon hispidus*
Foxglove	*Digitalis purpurea*
Yellow Rattle	*Rhinanthus minor*
Sneezewort	*Achillea ptarmica*
Agrimony	*Agrimonia eupatoria*

Fairy Flax	*Linum catharticum*
Clustered Bellflower	*Campanula glomerata*

Many of these flowers are familiar from Pennine grassland over carboniferous limestone. The mild climate of the magnesian limestone is reflected in the presence of the two species of *Clinopodium*. Wild Basil is an aromatic culinary herb which is generally distributed on calcareous soils across Yorkshire. Common Calamint *(Clinopodium ascendens)* is much commoner in the south and takes advantage of the mild habitat to travel north. This sweet-smelling herb was once used to hide the flavour of bad meat. There are several naturalised garden escapes in the ground, apart from the Pink and Wallflower of the actual ruins. Several manificent plants of Martagon Lily *(Lilium martagon)* grow in the grassland beside the path and Welsh Poppy *(Mecanopsis cambrica)* is a successful opportunist that will seed into any open pockets of soil. Naturalised Canadian Golden Rod *(Solidago canadensis)* and London Pride *(Saxifraga umbrosa)* complete our list for the grounds. A visit to Fountains Abbey is a must for any naturalist who finds himself in the neighbourhood of this famous ancient ruin.

The original building stone for both Jervaux and Fountains was excavated from local quarries. These quarries are excellent habitats in which to study the characteristic magnesian limestone flora. When such quarries have remained undisturbed for a long period the wild orchid flora is likely to be rich.
Species to look for include:-

Pyramid Orchid	*Anacamptis pyramidalis*
Fragrant Orchid	*Gymnadenia conopsea*
Common Spotted Orchid	*Dactylorhiza fuchsii*
Common Twayblade	*Listera ovata*
Bee Orchid	*Ophrys apifera*

Squinancywort *(Asperula cynanchica* plate 12b*)* can be found here. These delicate pink flowers are common members of the southern calcareous communities but become rare in Yorkshire. The encroaching grassland on a south-facing abandoned quarry is an ideal home for this tiny Bedstraw.

From the high peaks in the west to the magnesian limestone lowlands of the east, the artificial habitats available for flowers cover the whole range of man's activities. Whether it be railway, mine spoil or quarry face these habitats form important wild refuges for the characteristic flora of their particular neighbourhood.

FACTS AND FICTION

Welsh Poppy *(Mecanopsis cambrica).*
This species is a British native that used to be restricted to Wales and South-West England. The flower became popular in gardens, and seeding readily has escaped from the garden and become quite common in the wild. The generic name in Greek means bearing a resemblance to a poppy.

Martagon Lily *(Lilium martagon).*
Although this lily may possibly be native in southern England it is introduced elsewhere. In France it is now a protected species. In olden times the bulbs were thought to be a lucky talisman and were threaded into necklaces which were given to babies to keep witches away.

Himalayan Balsam *(Impatiens glandulifera).*
Also called Policeman's Helmet. The plant was introduced into Britain in the middle of the last century. It escaped and spread rapidly and is now abundant in the north of England, particularly on river banks. The explosive fruit can throw the seeds a long way and this has helped the plant to spread so quickly. The species has become an aggressive pest, shading out our native species.

PLATE xii
Pyramid Orchid *(Anacamptis pyramidalis).*

ACCESS AND NATURE RESERVES

Grass Wood. Reserve of the Yorkshire Wildlife Trust (Y.W.T.) SD 995651. Limestone woodland, grassland and cliff flora.

Globe Flower Wood. Y.W.T. SD 873667. Small, walled, ungrazed reserve with rich limestone flora.

Tow Hill. Y.W.T. SD 827871. Limestone pavement.

South House Pavement. Y.W.T. SD 776744. Limestone pavement.

Burton Leonard Lime Quarry. Y.W.T. SE 324630. Magnesian limestone quarry with grassland and woodland.

Yellands Meadow. Y.W.T. SD 918977. Typical Swaledale hay meadow.

Leyburn Old Glebe Field. Y.W.T. SE 102896. Magnesian limestone meadow with a rich flora.

Jervaux Abbey. SE 165850. The ruins have a very good range of magnesian limestone plants.

Fountains Abbey and grounds. SE 2768. National Trust with entrance charge. Limestone grassland, woodland, aquatic and old ruin flora.

Colt Park Wood. SD 775770. National Nature Reserve where permit is needed. Limestone pavement and Ash woodland.

Ling Gill. SD 803778. National Nature Reserve. Steep-wooded limestone ravine.

Malham Tarn. SD 890672. Field Studies Council and National Trust. Permit needed off the public rights of way. Calcareous tarn, bog and fen.

Scar Close. SD 753775. National Nature Reserve where permit is needed. Limestone pavement.

Upper Teesdale. National Nature Reserve. NY 8528. Limestone grassland and streamside vegetation with grouse moor.

Gouthwaite Reservoir. SE 1367. Reserve of the Yorkshire Water Authority.

Scar House Reservoir. SE 0777. Private road of Yorkshire Water Authority from Middlesmoor; entrance charge.

Pennine Way. 160 Km. long distance way which crosses the Yorkshire Dales.

In respect of the Yorkshire Wildlife Trust Reserves, visiting permits, further information and applications for membership can be obtained from the Y.W.T., 10 Toft Green, Micklegate, York.

GENERAL REFERENCES AND SOURCES FOR FACTS AND FICTION

Aichele, D. — 'Wild Flowers, a Field Guide in Colour'. Octopus, 1976.

Arnold, S. M. — 'A Simple Field Key to Common British Wild Flowers'. The Author. 1983.

Arnold, S. M. — 'Wild Flowers of the Yorkshire Wolds'. Hutton Press, 1985.

Arnold, S. M. — 'Wild Flowers of the North York Moors National Park'. Hutton Press, 1986.

Baines, H. — 'The Flora of Yorkshire'. Longman, Orme, Brown, Green Longman, 1840.

Clapham, A. R.,ed. — 'Upper Teesdale'. Collins, 1978.

Culpepper, T. — 'Culpepper's Complete Herbal and English Physician'. Facsimile of 1862 ed. Harvey Sales, 1981.

Gordon, L. — 'A Country Herbal'. Webb and Bower, 1980.

Hartley, M. and Ingilby J. — 'The Yorkshire Dales'. Dent and Sons, 1956.

Lacey, W. S. ed. — 'Britain's National Parks'. Windward Antler Books, 1984.

Mabey, R. — 'Food for Free'. Collins, 1972.

Nilson, S. — 'Orchids of Northern Europe'. Penguin Nature Guides, 1979.

Reader's Digest — 'Field Guide to the Wild Flowers of Britain'. 1981.

Richardson, R. — 'Hedgerow Cookery'. Penguin Books, 1980.

Shaw, J. G. — 'The Geology around Malham Tarn'. Field Studies Council, Occasional Publication No.3, 1982.

Sloover, J. and Goossens, M. — 'Wild Herbs : a Field Guide'. David and Charles.

'Yorkshire Dales National Park' — H.M.S.O., Guide No.9, 1971.

INDEX

Numbers in **bold** refer to illustrations